Step Forward

Language for Everyday Life

SERIES DIRECTOR
Jayme Adelson-Goldstein

Introductory Level

Jenni Currie Santamaria

OXFORD
UNIVERSITY PRESS

OXFORD
UNIVERSITY PRESS

198 Madison Avenue
New York, NY 10016 USA

Great Clarendon Street, Oxford OX2 6DP UK

Oxford University Press is a department of the University of Oxford.
It furthers the University's objective of excellence in research, scholarship,
and education by publishing worldwide in

Oxford New York

Auckland Cape Town Dar es Salaam Hong Kong Karachi
Kuala Lumpur Madrid Melbourne Mexico City Nairobi
New Delhi Shanghai Taipei Toronto

With offices in

Argentina Austria Brazil Chile Czech Republic France Greece
Guatemala Hungary Italy Japan Poland Portugal Singapore
South Korea Switzerland Thailand Turkey Ukraine Vietnam

OXFORD and OXFORD ENGLISH are registered trademarks of
Oxford University Press

© Oxford University Press 2008

Database right Oxford University Press (maker)

Library of Congress Cataloging-in-Publication Data
Adelson-Goldstein, Jayme.
Step Forward : language for everyday life / series director: Jayme Adelson-
Goldstein; intro.: Jenni Currie Santamaria
     p. cm.
  Includes index.
  ISBN 978-0-19-439843-5 (pbk. : student bk : introductory level) 1. English
language–Textbooks for foreign speakers. 2. Adult education. I. Santamaria,
Jenni Currie. II. Title.
  PE1128.A34 2007.
  428.2'4–dc22

                              2007016227

Editorial Director: Sally Yagan
Senior Publishing Manager: Stephanie Karras
Head of Project and Development Editors: Karen Horton
Managing Editor: Sharon Sargent
Associate Project Editor: Meredith Stoll
Design Director: Robert Carangelo
Design Project Manager: Maj-Britt Hagsted
Project Manager: Allison Harm
Senior Designer: Claudia Carlson
Production Layout Artist: Julie Armstrong
Production Manager: Shanta Persaud
Production Controller: Eve Wong
Packager: Bill Smith Studio

ISBN: 978 0 19 439843 5

Printed in Hong Kong

10 9 8 7 6 5 4 3 2 1

ACKNOWLEDGMENTS

Cover photograph: Corbis/Punchstock
Back cover photograph: Brian Rose
Illustrations by: Shawn Banner, p. 21, p. 49, p. 60, p. 84, p. 97, p. 112, p. 124 (bottom),
p. 125 (top), p. 144; Barbara Bastian, p. 44, p. 118; Kenneth Batelman, p. 29, p. 38, p.
65, p. 89, p. 110, p. 131; John Batten, p. 23, p. 34, p. 54, p. 70, p. 102, p. 109, p. 114, p.
138; Kathy Baxendale, p. 32, p. 36, p. 100, p. 105, p. 111, p.128; Bill Smith Studio, p.
4; Annie Bissett, p. 123 (bottom); Arlene Boehm, p. 2, p. 10, p. 45, p. 66, p. 89, p. 101,
p. 148; Kevin Brown, p. 7, p. 37, p. 42, p. 88, p. 90, p. 124 (top and middle), p. 130,
p. 135; Gary Bullock, p. 9, p. 33, p. 57; Richard Carbajal, p. 22, p. 41, p. 49, p. 63, p.
100, p. 111, p. 135; Laurie Α. Conley, p. 30, p. 78, p. 141, p. 150; Mona Daly, p. 61; Bill
Dickson, p. 24, p. 58, p. 82, p. 85, p. 112, p. 121, p. 142; Jody Emery, p. 40, p. 62, p. 75,
p. 98, p. 113, p. 123 (top), p. 137; Colin Hayes, p. 4, p. 26, p. 41, p. 86, p. 101, p. 134;
Kevin Hopgood, p. 14, p. 31, p. 62, p. 91, p. 127, p. 146; Jay Mazhar, p. 6, p. 86, p. 106,
p. 110, p. 134; Karen Minot, p. 125 (middle); Marc Mones, p. 11, p. 25, p. 35, p. 76, p.
107, p. 136; Jay Montgomery, p. 116; Terry Paczko, p. 56, p. 63, p. 80, p. 104, p. 177, p.
138; Pamorama.com, p. 5, p. 7, p. 12, p. 13, p. 39, p. 71, p. 132, p. 136; Geo Parkin, p.
20, p. 21, p. 38, p. 55, p. 79, p. 115, p. 122, p. 139; Roger Penwill, p. 19, p. 43, p. 67, p.
103, p. 151; Pixelation Digital Imagery, p. 2, p. 5, p. 7, p. 17, p. 28, p. 29, p. 41, p. 53, p.
64, p. 65, p. 77, p. 89, p. 95, p. 99, p. 111, p. 137, p. 143, p. 147, p. 149; Karen Pritchett,
p. 8, p. 68, p. 92, p. 93; Marthe Roberts, p. 48, p. 52, p. 87, p. 113; Don Stewart, p.
69; William Waitzman, p. 16, p. 18, p. 46, p. 64, p. 94, p. 112, p. 120, p. 135; Graham
White, p. 126; Simon Williams, p. 60, p. 81, p. 129, p. 132, p. 140; Ron Zalme, p. 26, p.
50, p. 52, p. 72, p. 74, p. 88, p. 93, p. 98, p. 108.

Photographs: Tony Anderson/Getty Images, p. 73; Christine Balderas/iStockphoto, p.
12 (center right), p. 17 (center left), (top right), p. 30; Big House Productions/Getty
Images, p. 144; Blend Images/Alamy, p. 12 (bottom left), p. 73; Bloomimage/Corbis,
p. 30; ©Brand X Pictures/Alamy, p. 64 (bottom right); Keith Brofsky/Getty Images,
p. 148; Bubbles Photolibrary/Alamy, p. 96 (bottom right); Ron Chapple/Jupiter
Images, p. 83; Comstock Images/Jupiter Images, p. 95; Kitt Cooper-Smith/Alamy, p.
40; Corbis/Jupiter Images, p. 3 (center left); Dennis Kitchen Photography, p. 3 (top
right), (center right), (bottom center), p. 17 (bottom left), p. 96, p. 145; Mary Kate
Denny/ PhotoEdit, p. 148; Kevin Dodge/Corbis, p. 76; Mark Downey/Getty Images,
p. 144; Dynamic Graphics, Inc./Jupiter Images, p. 3 (bottom left); Christoph Ermel/
iStockphoto, p. 40; FredS/iStockphoto, p. 12 (top right); Getty Images/Blend Images,
p. 12 (bottom right); Jaume Gual/age footstock, p. 30; Hill Street Studios/age
footstock, p. 144; Jack Hollingsworth/Getty Images, p. 47; Zigy Kaluzny/Getty Images,
p. 148; Bonnie Kamin/PhotoEdit, p. 40; I and I/Masterfile, p. 75; Jupiter Images,
p. 143; Jutta Klee/Corbis, p. 73; Ruediger Knoblock/A. B./zefa/Corbis, p. 133; Mark
Leibowitz/Masterfile. p. 73; Robert Manella/Comstock/Corbis, p. 76; Felicia Martinez/
PhotoEdit, p. 17 (top left); Gib Martinez/Alamy, p. 40; Masterfile/Royalty Free, p. 76;
©Neil McAllister/Alamy, p. 64 (bottom left); Ryan McVay/Getty Images, p. 23, p. 35,
p. 119; Amos Morgan/Getty Images, p. 10; Paul Morley/Shutterstock, p. 3 (top left);
Gala Narezo/Getty Images, p. 75; Richard T. Nowitz/Corbis, p. 76; Gabe Palmer/Alamy
p. 12 (top left); Michael N. Paras/age footstock, p. 75; Jose Luis Pelaez Inc./Jupiter
Images, p. 75; Barbara Penoyar/Getty Images, p. 59, p. 131; Michael Poehlman/Getty
Images, p. 96 (bottom left); Mike Powell, p. 30; Lorne Resnick/age footstock, p. 144;
Royalty-Free/Corbis, p. 75; Bob Thomas/Getty Images, p. 12 (center left); T Stock
Free/Jupiter Images, p. 107; Pierre Tremblay/Masterfile, p. 148; David Young-Wolff/
PhotoEdit, p. 3 (bottom right).

We gratefully acknowledge the collaborative spirit, dedication
and skill of the *Step Forward Intro* editorial and design team:
Stephanie Karras, Sharon Sargent, Ellen Northcutt, Meredith
Stoll, Meg Araneo, Maj-Britt Hagsted and Bill Smith Studio.
We also want to express our deep appreciation to our students
and colleagues who inspire us on a daily basis.
Jenni Currie Santamaria
Jayme Adelson-Goldstein

Oceans of gratitude to Sharon Sargent, whose dedication to
"getting it right" can be seen on every page of this book, and to
Jayme Adelson-Goldstein for her insightful leadership.

For Tony and Amaya, my bedrock.
–Jennie Currie Santamaria

My heartfelt thanks to the wondrous Jennie Currie Santamaria
whose commitment to the learner never falters. I also thank
Kathy Santopietro Weddel for her many insights and "level
vigilance."
–Jayme

ACKNOWLEDGMENTS

Curriculum Consultant
Kathy Santopietro Weddel
Northern Colorado Literacy Program, Littleton, CO

The Publisher and Series Director would like to acknowledge the following individuals for their invaluable input during the development of this series:

Robert Anzelde Triton College, River Grove, IL

Patricia Bell Lake Technical Center, Eustis, FL

Curtis Bonney North Seattle Community College, Seattle, WA

Ana Patricia Castro Harvest English Institute, Newark, NJ

Edwidge Bryant University of North Florida, Jacksonville, FL

Julie Caspersen Old Marshall Adult Education Center, Sacramento, CA

Bart Chaney Dallas Independent School District, Dallas, TX

Kathleen Fallon Clackamas Community College, Oregon City, OR

Cheryl L. Fuentes ESOL Consultant, Alexandria, VA

Carol Garcia College of DuPage, Glen Ellyn, IL

Ann Jackson Mid Florida Tech, Orlando, FL

Gaye Kendall Harris County Department of Education, Houston, TX

Jennifer Martin Baldwin Park Adult and Community Education, Baldwin Park, CA

Suzi Monti Community College of Baltimore County, Baltimore, MD

Rob Patton Communities in Schools—Central Texas, Austin, TX

Linda A. Pelc New York City Department of Education, New York, NY

Marvina Pérez Hooper Lake Technical Center, Eustis, FL

David L. Red Fairfax County Public Schools, Falls Church, VA

Barbara Sample Spring Institute for Intercultural Learning, Denver, CO

Denise Selleck City College of San Francisco—Alemany, San Francisco, CA

Esther Shupe Brookdale Community College, Long Branch, NJ

Margaret B. Silver English Language and Literacy Center, Clayton, MO

Melissa Singler Cape Fear Community College, Wilmington, NC

Betty Stone Somerville Center for Adult Learning Experiences, Somerville, MA

Maliheh Vafai Overfelt Adult Center, San Jose, CA

Cynthia Wiseman Borough of Manhattan Community College, New York, NY

We would also like to thank the following students in the Fall 2006 Beginning Literacy Class at ABC Adult School in Cerritos, CA.

Emelia Alvarez
Virej Benyamin
Liang-Ming Chen
Li Yu Chen
Yang Ja Choi
Soon Hee Chong
Chi-Yu Chou Chiu
Lotai Chung
Somath Oeurn Dell
Adulfo Garcia
Kyung Soon Han
Shu-yeh Hsu
Hee Sik Im
Jin Taek Jung

Jung Soon Jung
Jin Shik Kim
Kil Su Kim
Soon Hi Kim
Soon Yi Kim
In Taek Lee
Jung So Lee
Myung Yong Lee
Ok Ja Lee
Tae Soo Lee
Wan Chen Lee
Phourngmalay Long
Vanny Long
David Lopez

Maria Luisa Lopez
Kai Pang Ng
Ga Young Oh
Oknyu Park
Sun Soon Park
Sung Ja Park
Young Sun Park
Norma Talavera Riviera
Zaihong Shen
Angelica Torres
Min Chen Wang
Tzu Tseng Wang
Keum Soon Woo
Young Ja Yoo

TABLE OF CONTENTS

Unit	Life Skills & Civics Competencies	Vocabulary	Grammar	Critical Thinking & Math Concepts	Reading & Writing
Pre-unit **The First Step** **page 2**	• Respond to basic classroom directions • Say and spell names • Identify and read phone numbers • Introduce yourself	• Names • Numbers • Classroom items	• Imperatives	• Read, write, and identify numbers 0–100 • Identify and read phone numbers	• Identify letters of the alphabet • Read and write numbers 0–100
Unit 1 **Nice to Meet You** **page 8**	• Follow classroom directions • Respond to simple commands • Give personal information • Practice social conversations	• Classroom directions • Classroom items	• Subject pronouns • Statements with *be* • *A* or *an*	• Differentiate between first, middle, and last names **Problem solving:** • Ask for help in the classroom	• Write personal information • Write about the classroom • Read a class supplies list
Unit 2 **How are you feeling?** **page 20**	• Talk about feelings • Ask and respond to personal information questions • Express regret • Read a form • Read an envelope	• Feelings • Items on a form • Parts of an address	• Negative statements with *be* • Contractions with *be*	• Reflect on feelings **Problem solving:** • Determine how to find a correct zip code	• Read about personal information • Give personal information • Write sentences using contractions • Read and complete a form • Read an envelope
Unit 3 **What time is it?** **page 32**	• Interpret clock times • Identify places in the community • Listen for and ask about the time • Ask for information about places in the community • Interpret a bus schedule	• Time • Places in the community • Transportation	• *Yes/No* questions with *be* • Short answers with *be*	• Interpret clock times • Interpret a bus schedule **Problem solving:** • Identify ways to solve a scheduling conflict	• Write *Yes/No* questions • Write short answers with *be* • Read a bus schedule

Listening & Speaking	CASAS Step Forward Introductory Level Student Book	Standardized Student Syllabi/LCPs	SCANS Competencies	EFF Content Standards
• Listen to basic classroom directions • Say and spell names • Listen and say telephone numbers • Listen for plurals • Introduce yourself • Talk about the classroom	**L1:** 0.1.2 **L2:** 0.12, 0.1.5, 6.0.1 **L3:** 0.1.2, 0.1.4, 0.1.5	• **L1:** 1.15.07, 1.17.01, 1.17.02 • **L2:** 1.06.01 • **L3:** 1.05.01, 1.15.02	Most SCANS are incorporated into this unit, with an emphasis on: • Participating as a Member of a Team • Acquiring and Evaluating Information • Interpreting and Communicating Information • Reading • Seeing Things in the Mind's Eye • Speaking	Most EFFs are incorporated into this unit, with an emphasis on: • Listen actively • Observing critically • Cooperate with others • Speaking so others can understand • Reading with understanding
• Listen to classroom directions • Talk about the classroom • Give personal information • Practice social conversations • Listen for *a* or *an* **Pronunciation:** • Differentiate between *i* and *e*	**L1:** 0.1.2, 0.1.5, 7.4.5 **L2:** 0.1.2, 0.1.4, 0.2.1 **L3:** 0.1.2, 7.4.7 **L4:** 0.1.2, 0.1.4, 0.2.1, 7.4.7 **L5:** 0.1.2 **RE:** 0.1.2, 0.1.5, 7.4.5, 7.4.7	**L1:** 1.15.07, 1.15.08 **L2:** 1.15.02 **L3:** 1.15.06, 1.15.08, 1.16.01 **L4:** 1.05.01, 1.15.02, 1.15.08, 1.17.02 **L5:** 1.15.07, 1.15.08, 1.16.09 **RE:** 1.15.07, 1.16.01	Most SCANS are incorporated into this unit, with an emphasis on: • Participating as a member of a team • Interpreting and communicating information • Seeing things in the mind's eye • Knowing how to learn • Problem solving • Listening • Reading	Most EFFs are incorporated into this unit, with an emphasis on: • Listening actively • Speaking so others can understand • Cooperating with others • Reading with understanding • Solving problems and making decisions • Observing critically
• Talk about feelings • Listen for personal information • Respond to personal information questions • Express regret **Pronunciation:** • Listen for syllables	**L1:** 0.1.2, 0.1.5, 7.4.5 **L2:** 0.1.2, 0.1.4, 0.2.1 **L3:** 0.1.2, 7.4.7 **L4:** 0.1.2, 0.1.4, 0.2.1, 7.4.7 **L5:** 0.1.2, 0.2.2, 7.4.7 **RE:** 0.1.2, 0.1.5, 7.3.1, 7.3.2, 7.4.5	**L1:** 1.15.02 **L2:** 1.15.02 **L3:** 1.15.06, 1.15.08, 1.16.11 **L4:** 1.05.03, 1.15.08 **L5:** 1.05.02, 1.15.05, 1.15.08 **RE:** 1.16.11	Most SCANS are incorporated into this unit, with an emphasis on: • Participating as a member of a team • Interpreting and communicating information • Seeing things in the mind's eye • Knowing how to learn • Problem solving • Listening • Reading	Most EFFs are incorporated into this unit, with an emphasis on: • Listening actively • Speaking so others can understand • Cooperating with others • Reading with understanding • Solving problems and making decisions • Reflecting and evaluating • Learning through research • Observing critically
• Listen for *a.m.* and *p.m.* • Listen for and ask about the time • Ask for information about places in the community **Pronunciation:** • *Yes/No* question intonation	**L1:** 0.1.2, 0.1.5, 2.3.1, 7.4.5 **L2:** 0.1.2, 0.2.1, 7.4.7 **L3:** 0.1.2, 0.1.4, 7.4.7 **L4:** 0.1.2, 0.1.4, 0.2.1, 7.4.7 **L5:** 0 .1.2, 0.1.5, 2.2.4, 7.4.7 **RE:** 0.1.2, 0.1.5, 7.3.1, 7.3.2, 7.4.5, 7.4.7	**L1:** 1.08.02, 1.15.07 **L2:** 1.15.02 **L3:** 1.15.08 **L4:** 1.05.01, 1.15.08 **L5:** 1.15.08 **RE:** 1.15.08	Most SCANS are incorporated into this unit, with an emphasis on: • Participating as a member of a team • Interpreting and communicating information • Knowing how to learn • Problem solving • Time • Seeing things in the mind's eye • Listening • Reading	Most EFFs are incorporated into this unit, with an emphasis on: • Listening actively • Speaking so others can understand • Cooperating with others • Reading with understanding • Solving problems and making decisions • Convey ideas in writing • Learning through research

Listening & Speaking	CASAS Step Forward Introductory Level Student Book	Standardized Student Syllabi/LCPs	SCANS Competencies	EFF Content Standards
• Listen for days, months, years, and dates • Talk about the days of the week • Respond to information questions • Say goodbye appropriately **Pronunciation:** • Differentiate between *t* and *th*	**L1:** 0.1.2, 0.1.5, 7.4.5 **L2:** 0.1.2, 7.4.7 **L3:** 0.1.2, 0.2.3, 7.4.7 **L4:** 0.1.2, 0.1.4, 0.1.5, 7.4.7 **L5:** 0.1.2, 0.1.5, 7.4.7 **RE:** 0.1.2, 0.1.5, 7.3.1, 7.3.2, 7.4.5, 7.4.7	• **L1:** 1.05.01, 1.15.07 • **L2:** 1.05.02, 1.15.08 • **L3:** 1.15.08, 1.16.08 • **L4:** 1.05.01, 1.15.08, 1.17.02 • **L5:** 1.08.01, 1.15.08 • **RE:** 1.15.08, 1.16.08	Most SCANS are incorporated into this unit, with an emphasis on: • Participating as a member of a team • Interpreting and communicating information • Seeing things in the mind's eye • Knowing how to learn • Problem solving • Listening • Reading	Most EFFs are incorporated into this unit, with an emphasis on: • Listening actively • Speaking so others can understand • Cooperating with others • Reading with understanding • Solving problems and making decisions • Observing critically • Reflecting and evaluating • Conveying ideas in writing • Learning through research
• Listen for and talk about prices • Listen for change amounts	**L1:** 0.1.2, 0.1.5, 7.4.5, 7.4.7 **L2:** 0.1.2 **L3:** 0.1.2, 7.4.7 **L4:** 0.1.2, 6.2.3, 7.4.7 **L5:** 0.1.2, 7.4.7 **RE:** 0.1.2, 0.1.5, 7.3.1, 7.3.2, 7.4.5, 7.4.7	**L1:** 1.08.05, 1.15.08 **L2:** 1.08.05, 1.11.01 **L3:** 1.15.06, 1.15.08 **L4:** 1.08.05, 1.11.01, 1.11.03, 1.15.08 **L5:** 1.08.07, 1.15.08 **RE:** 1.15.08	Most SCANS are incorporated into this unit, with an emphasis on: • Participating as a member of a team • Interpreting and communicating information • Arithmetic/Mathematics • Problem solving • Money • Listening • Seeing things in the mind's eye • Reading	Most EFFs are incorporated into this unit, with an emphasis on: • Listening actively • Using math to solve problems and communicate • Cooperating with others • Reading with understanding • Solving problems and making decisions • Observing critically • Conveying ideas in writing • Reflecting and evaluating
• Talk about family members and friends • Listen for marital status and titles	**L1:** 0.1.2, 0.1.5, 0.1.6, 7.4.5 **L2:** 0.1.2, 7.4.7 **L3:** 0.1.2, 7.4.7 **L4:** 0.1.2, 0.1.4, 6.6.4, 7.4.7 **L5:** 7.4.7 **RE:** 0.1.2, 0.1.5, 7.3.1, 7.3.2, 7.4.5, 7.4.7	**L1:** 1.14.01, 1.15.07 **L2:** 1.14.01, 1.15.08 **L3:** 1.15.06, 1.15.08, 1.16.10 **L4:** 1.15.08 **L5:** 1.15.08 **RE:** 1.15.08	Most SCANS are incorporated into this unit, with an emphasis on: • Participating as a member of a team • Interpreting and communicating information • Knowing how to learn • Problem solving • Arithmetic/Mathematics • Listening • Seeing things in the mind's eye • Reading	Most EFFs are incorporated into this unit, with an emphasis on: • Listening actively • Cooperating with others • Reading with understanding • Solving problems and making decisions • Using math to solve problems and communicate • Conveying ideas in writing • Reflecting and evaluating

Listening & Speaking	CASAS Step Forward Introductory Level Student Book	Standardized Student Syllabi/LCPs	SCANS Competencies	EFF Content Standards
• Describe food preferences • Ask for help in a store • Listen for prices	**L1:** 0.1.2, 0.1.5, 7.4.5 **L2:** 0.1.2, 7.4.7 **L3:** 0.1.2, 7.4.7 **L4:** 0.1.2, 0.1.4, 0.1.5, 6.1.3 **L5:** 7.4.7 **RE:** 0.1.2, 0.1.5, 7.3.1, 7.3.2, 7.4.5, 7.4.7	**L1:** 1.07.06 **L2:** 1.15.08 **L3:** 1.15.06, 1.15.08, 1.16.02 **L4:** 1.05.01 **L5:** 1.15.08 **RE:** 1.15.08	Most SCANS are incorporated into this unit, with an emphasis on: • Participating as a member of a team • Interpreting and communicating information • Seeing things in the mind's eye • Arithmetic/Mathematics • Problem solving • Listening • Reading	Most EFFs are incorporated into this unit, with an emphasis on: • Listening actively • Speaking so others can understand • Using math to solve problems and communicate • Reading with understanding • Solving problems and making decisions • Conveying ideas in writing • Learning through research • Reflecting and evaluating
• Talk about parts of the body • Listen for and check problems on a medical history form • Make medical appointments • Listen for medical appointment information **Pronunciation:** • Differentiate between *a* sounds	**L1:** 0.1.2, 0.1.5, 7.4.5 **L2:** 0.1.2, 3.1.1, 3.2.1 **L3:** 0.1.2 **L4:** 0.1.2, 0.1.4 **L5:** 3.3.1, 7.4.7 **RE:** 0.1.2, 0.1.5, 7.3.1, 7.3.2, 7.4.5, 7.4.7	**L1:** 1.07.01, 1.15.07 **L2:** 1.07.02 **L3:** 1.07.02, 1.15.06 **L4:** 1.17.01 **L5:** 1.07.04, 1.15.08 **RE:** 1.15.08	Most SCANS are incorporated into this unit, with an emphasis on: • Participating as a member of a team • Interpreting and communicating information • Seeing things in the mind's eye • Knowing how to learn • Problem solving • Listening • Arithmetic/Mathematics • Reading	Most EFFs are incorporated into this unit, with an emphasis on: • Listening actively • Speaking so others can understand • Cooperating with others • Reading with understanding • Solving problems and making decisions • Conveying ideas in writing • Learning through research • Reflecting and evaluating
• Talk about colors • Listen for clothing sizes and prices • State weather conditions	**L1:** 0.1.2, 0.1.5, 7.4.5 **L2:** 0.1.2, 7.4.7 **L3:** 0.1.2, 7.4.7 **L4:** 0.1.2, 1.2.1, 6.2.1, 7.4.7 **L5:** 2.3.3, 7.4.7 **RE:** 0.1.2, 0.1.5, 7.3.1, 7.3.2, 7.4.5, 7.4.7	**L1:** 1.15.07 **L2:** 1.15.08 **L3:** 1.15.06, 1.15.08, 1.16.02 **L4:** 1.11.03, 1.11.04, 1.15.08 **L5:** 1.15.06, 1.15.08 **RE:** 1.15.08	Most SCANS are incorporated into this unit, with an emphasis on: • Participating as a member of a team • Interpreting and communicating information • Applying technology to task • Arithmetic/Mathematics • Problem solving • Seeing things in the mind's eye • Listening • Reading	Most EFFs are incorporated into this unit, with an emphasis on: • Listening actively • Using math to solve problems and communicate • Cooperating with others • Using information and communication technology • Solving problems and making decisions • Conveying ideas in writing • Learning through research • Reflecting and evaluating

Unit	Life Skills & Civics Competencies	Vocabulary	Grammar	Critical Thinking & Math Concepts	Reading & Writing
Unit 10 **Where's the bank?** **page 116**	• Identify places in the community • Ask for and give locations • Read a simple map • Distinguish between emergencies and non-emergencies • Read a city-services directory	• Places in the community • Locations • Community services	• Statements with *There is* and *There are* • Ask and answer *Yes/No* questions with *Is there*	• Ask for and give locations • Distinguish between emergencies and non-emergencies **Real-life math:** • Determine distance between points on a map **Problem solving:** • Decide what to do with noisy neighbors	• Read and write about locations in the community • Write *Yes/No* questions with *Is there* and answers • Read a simple map • Read a city-services directory
Unit 11 **This Is My Home** **page 128**	• Identify places and things in the home • State the location of things in the home • Ask about a home for rent • Identify different types of housing • Interpret housing ads	• Home furnishings • Rooms in the home • Types of housing	• Prepositions of location • Possessives with *'s* • Ask and answer questions with *How many*	• Interpret classified housing ads **Real-life math:** • Calculate the first month's payment for an apartment **Problem solving:** • Decide what to do when electric power is out	• Read and write about the home • Write questions with *How many* and answers • Read housing ads
Unit 12 **Yes, I can!** **page 140**	• Identify common occupations • Identify skills required for a job • Respond to basic job-interview questions • Interpret job ads	• Occupations • Job skills	• Statements with *can* and *can't* • *Yes/No* questions and answers with *can* and *can't*	• Interpret help-wanted ads **Problem solving:** • Determine how to handle a conflict between social and work obligations	• Read and write about job skills • Write sentences with *can* and *can't* • Read job ads

Listening & Speaking	CASAS Step Forward Introductory Level Student Book	Standardized Student Syllabi/LCPs	SCANS Competencies	EFF Content Standards
Talk about places in a community Listen for locations Ask for and give locations	**L1:** 0.1.2, 0.1.5, 7.4.5 **L2:** 0.1.2, 1.1.3 **L3:** 7.4.7 **L4:** 0.1.2, 0.1.4, 1.1.3, 6.1.1 **L5:** 0.1.5, 2.1.2, 7.4.7 **RE:** 0.1.2, 0.1.5, 7.3.1, 7.3.2, 7.4.5, 7.4.7	**L1:** 1.15.07 **L2:** 1.09.03 **L3:** 1.15.06, 1.15.08 **L4:** 1.09.03 **L5:** 1.12.02, 1.15.08 **RE:** 1.15.08	Most SCANS are incorporated into this unit, with an emphasis on: • Participating as a member of a team • Interpreting and communicating information • Seeing things in the mind's eye • Knowing how to learn • Problem solving • Listening • Arithmetic/Mathematics • Reading	Most EFFs are incorporated into this unit, with an emphasis on: • Listening actively • Speaking so others can understand • Cooperating with others • Reading with understanding • Solving problems and making decisions • Conveying ideas in writing • Learning through research • Using math to solve problems and communicate • Reflecting and evaluating
Talk about objects in the home Listen for information about things in the home Ask about a home for rent Listen for housing information	**L1:** 0.1.2, 0.1.5, 7.4.5 **L2:** 0.1.2 **L3:** 0.1.2, 7.4.7 **L4:** 0.1.2, 0.1.4, 1.4.2, 6.1.1 **L5:** 1.4.2, 7.4.7 **RE:** 0.1.2, 0.1.5, 7.3.1, 7.3.2, 7.4.5, 7.4.7	**L1:** 1.15.07 **L2:** 1.05.02 **L3:** 1.15.06, 1.15.08, 1.16.10 **L4:** 1.11.08 **L5:** 1.11.08, 1.15.08 **RE:** 1.15.08	Most SCANS are incorporated into this unit, with an emphasis on: • Participating as a member of a team • Interpreting and communicating information • Seeing things in the mind's eye • Knowing how to learn • Problem solving • Listening • Arithmetic/Mathematics • Reading	Most EFFs are incorporated into this unit, with an emphasis on: • Listening actively • Speaking so others can understand • Cooperating with others • Reading with understanding • Solving problems and making decisions • Conveying ideas in writing • Learning through research • Using math to solve problems and communicate • Reflecting and evaluating
Talk about jobs Listen for information about job skills Respond to basic job-interview questions Listen to a work schedule **Pronunciation:** Differentiate between *can* and *can't*	**L1:** 0.1.2, 0.1.5, 7.4.5 **L2:** 0.1.2, 4.1.8 **L3:** 0.1.2 **L4:** 0.1.2, 0.2.1 **L5:** 4.1.3, 4.1.8, 7.4.7 **RE:** 0.1.2, 0.1.5, 7.3.1, 7.3.2, 7.4.5, 7.4.7	**L1:** 1.15.07 **L2:** 1.05.02 **L3:** 1.15.06 **L4:** 1.15.02, 1.17.02 **L5:** 1.01.07, 1.15.08 **RE:** 1.15.08	Most SCANS are incorporated into this unit, with an emphasis on: • Participating as a member of a team • Interpreting and communicating information • Seeing things in the mind's eye • Knowing how to learn • Problem solving • Listening	Most EFFs are incorporated into this unit, with an emphasis on: • Listening actively • Speaking so others can understand • Cooperating with others • Reading with understanding • Solving problems and making decisions • Conveying ideas in writing • Learning through research • Reflecting and evaluating

A Word or Two About Reading Introductions to Textbooks

Teaching professionals rarely read a book's introduction. Instead, we flip through the book's pages, using the pictures, topics, and exercises to determine whether the book matches our learners' needs and our teaching style. We scan the reading passages, conversations, writing tasks, and grammar charts to judge the authenticity and accuracy of the text. At a glance, we assess how easy it would be to manage the pair work, group activities, evaluations, and application tasks.

This Introduction, however, also offers valuable information for the teacher. Because you've read this far, I encourage you to read a little further to learn how *Step Forward's* key concepts, components, and multilevel applications will help you help your learners.

Step Forward's Key Concepts

Step Forward is...

- the instructional backbone for single-level and multilevel classrooms.
- a standards-based, performance-based, and topic-based series for low-beginning through high-intermediate learners.
- a source for ready-made, four-skill lesson plans that address the skills our learners need in their workplace, civic, personal, and academic lives.
- a collection of learner-centered, communicative English-language practice activities.

The classroom is a remarkable place. *Step Forward* respects the depth of experience and knowledge that learners bring to the learning process. At the same time, *Step Forward* recognizes that learners' varied proficiencies, goals, interests, and educational backgrounds create instructional challenges for teachers.

To ensure that our learners leave each class having made progress toward their language and life goals, *Step Forward* works from these key concepts:

- **The wide spectrum of learners' needs makes using materials that support multilevel instruction essential.** *Step Forward* works with single-level and multilevel classes.
- **Learners' prior knowledge is a valuable teaching tool.** Prior knowledge questions appear in every *Step Forward* lesson.

- **Learning objectives are the cornerstone of instruction.** Each *Step Forward* lesson focuses on an objective that derives from identified learner needs, correlates to state and federal standards, and connects to a meaningful communication task. Progress toward the objective is evaluated at the end of the lesson.
- **Vocabulary, grammar and pronunciation skills play an essential role in language learning. They provide learners with the tools needed to achieve life skill, civics, workplace, and academic competencies.** *Step Forward* includes strong vocabulary and grammar strands and features pronunciation and math lesson extensions in each unit.
- **Effective instruction requires a variety of instructional techniques and strategies to engage learners.** Techniques such as Early Production Questioning, Focused Listening, Total Physical Response (TPR), Cooperative Learning, and Problem Solving are embedded in the *Step Forward* series, along with grouping and classroom management strategies.

The *Step Forward* Program

The *Step Forward* program has five levels:

- Intro: pre-beginning
- Book 1: low-beginning
- Book 2: high-beginning
- Book 3: low-intermediate
- Book 4: intermediate to high-intermediate

Each level of *Step Forward* correlates to *The Oxford Picture Dictionary*. For pre-literacy learners, *The Basic Oxford Picture Dictionary Literacy Program* provides a flexible, needs-based approach to literacy instruction. Once learners develop literacy skills, they will be able to transition seamlessly into *Step Forward Student Book Introductory Level*.

Each *Step Forward* level includes the following components:

Step Forward Student Book

A collection of clear, engaging, four-skill lessons based on meaningful learning objectives.

Step Forward Audio Program

The recorded vocabulary, focused listening, conversations, pronunciation, and reading materials from the *Step Forward Student Book*.

Step Forward Step-By-Step Lesson Plans with Multilevel Grammar and Literacy Exercises CD-ROM

An instructional planning resource with interleaved *Step Forward Student Book* pages, featuring multilevel teaching strategies and teaching tips, and a CD-ROM of printable multilevel grammar and literacy practice.

Step Forward Workbook

Practice exercises for independent work in the classroom or as homework.

Step Forward Multilevel Activity Book

Photocopiable communicative practice activities and over 300 picture cards; lesson materials that work equally well in single-level or multilevel settings.

Step Forward Test Generator CD-ROM with ExamView® Assessment Suite

Hundreds of multiple choice and life-skill oriented test items for each *Step Forward Student Book*.

Step Forward Introductory Level also includes:

Step Forward Literacy Reproducible Book

Photocopiable fundamental skills practice for literacy-level students placed in the beginning classroom.

Multilevel Applications of *Step Forward*

All the *Step Forward* program components support multilevel instruction.

Step Forward is so named because it helps learners "step forward" toward their language and life goals, no matter where they start.

Regardless of level, all learners need materials that bolster comprehension with an appropriate amount of challenge. This makes multilevel materials an instructional necessity in most classrooms.

Each *Step Forward* lesson provides the following multilevel elements:

- **a general topic or competency area** that works across levels. This supports the concept that members of the class community need to feel connected, despite their differing abilities.
- **clear, colorful visuals and realia** that provide pre-level and on-level support during introduction,

presentation and practice exercises, as well as prompts for higher-level questions and exercises. In addition, *Step Forward* correlates to *The Oxford Picture Dictionary* so that teachers can use the visuals and vocabulary from *The Oxford Picture Dictionary* to support and expand upon each lesson.

- **learner-centered practice exercises** that can be used with same-level or mixed-level pairs or small groups. *Step Forward* exercises are broken down to their simplest steps. Once the exercise has been modeled, learners can usually conduct the exercises themselves.
- **pre-level, on-level, and higher-level objectives for each lesson and the multilevel strategies** necessary to carry out the lesson. These objectives are featured in the *Step-By-Step Lesson Plans*.
- **the** *Step Forward Workbook* **and** *Multilevel Grammar and Literacy Exercises CD-ROM* provide excellent "wait time" activities for learners who complete an exercise early, thus solving a real issue in the multilevel class.
- **a variety of pair, whole class, and small group activities** in the *Step Forward Multilevel Activity Book*. These activities are perfect for same-level and mixed-level grouping.
- **customizable evaluation exercises** in the *Step Forward Test Generator CD-ROM with ExamView® Assessment Suite*. These exercises make it possible to create evaluations specific to each level in the class.

Professional Development

As instructors, we need to reflect on second language acquisition in order to build a repertoire of effective instructional strategies. The *Step Forward Professional Development Program* provides research-based teaching strategies, tasks, and activities for single- and multilevel classes.

About Writing an ESL Series

It's collaborative! *Step Forward* is the product of dialogs with hundreds of teachers and learners. The dynamic quality of language instruction makes it important to keep this dialog alive. As you use this book in your classes, I invite you to contact me or any member of the *Step Forward* authorial team with your questions or comments.

Jayme Adelson-Goldstein, Series Director
Stepforwardteam.us@oup.com

Step Forward: All you need to ensure your learners' success.
All the *Step Forward Student Books* follow this format.

LESSON 1: VOCABULARY teaches key words and phrases relevant to the unit topic, and provides conversation practice using the target vocabulary.

New vocabulary is introduced through vibrant art and listening texts.

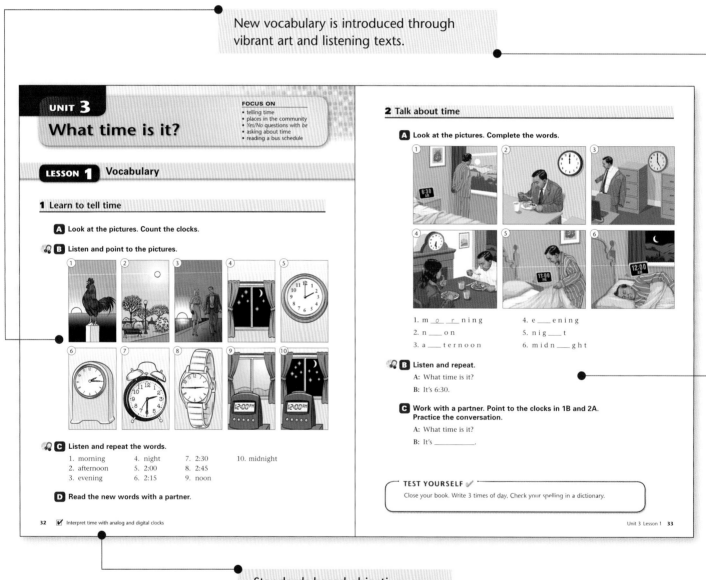

Standards-based objectives are identified at the beginning of every lesson for quick reference.

LESSON 2: LIFE STORIES expands on vocabulary learned in Lesson 1 and furthers learners' understanding through reading and writing about a life skills topic.

Life skills readings help learners practice the vocabulary in natural contexts.

Learners apply the vocabulary to their own lives by writing about their personal experiences.

LESSON 2 — Life stories

1 Read about places in the community

A Look at the pictures. Say the times.

8:00 Cindy
9:30
10:00
10:30
1:30
4:00
6:00

B Listen and repeat the words.

1. go to the store
2. go to the library
3. go to school
4. go to English class
5. go to work
6. go to the clinic
7. go home

C Listen and read Cindy's story.

1. I go to the store at 8:00.
2. I go to the library at 9:30.
3. I go to school at 10:00.
4. I go to English class at 10:30.

D Listen to Rick's story. Circle the correct word.

1. I go to ___ at 9:00.   (school)   the store
2. I go to ___ at 1:00.   the clinic   the library
3. I go to English ___ at 2:30. class   the clinic
4. I go to ___ at 6:00.   home   work   Rick

2 Write about your day

A Write about your day. Complete the sentences. Use your own ideas.

I go to _____ at _____.
I go to _____ at _____.
I go to English class at _____.

B Read your story to a partner.

3 Listen for *a.m.* and *p.m.*

A Look at the pictures. Read the times and sentences.

① 8 a.m. = 8:00 in the morning
I go to work at 8 a.m.

② 8 p.m. = 8:00 in the evening
I go home at 8 p.m.

B Listen. Circle *morning* or *evening*.

1. (morning)   evening   3. morning   evening
2. morning   evening   4. morning   evening

C Listen again. Write the times you hear.

1. _7 a.m._   2. _____   3. _____   4. _____

TEST YOURSELF ✔

Copy the sentences. Close your book. Then complete the sentences. Use your own ideas.

I go to _____ at _____ in the morning. I go _____ at _____ .

Test Yourself, at the end of every lesson, provides learners with ongoing self-assessment.

LESSON 3: GRAMMAR provides clear, simple presentation of the target structure followed by thorough, meaningful practice of it.

Clear grammar presentation and exercises help learners develop language confidence and accuracy.

Learners work together to increase fluency and accuracy, using the grammar point to talk about themselves.

LESSON 4: EVERYDAY CONVERSATION provides learners with fluent, authentic conversations to increase familiarity with natural English.

Pronunciation activities focus on common areas of difficulty.

Listening activities build listening skills.

Model dialogs feature authentic examples of everyday conversation.

LESSON 5: REAL-LIFE READING develops essential reading skills and offers life skill reading materials.

High-interest readings recycle vocabulary and grammar.

REVIEW AND EXPAND includes additional grammar practice and communicative group tasks to ensure your learners' progress.

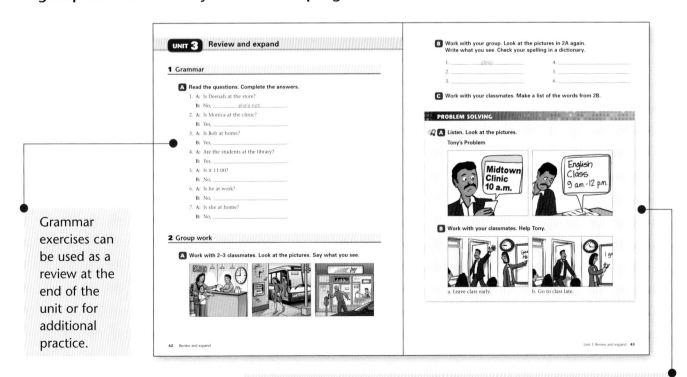

Grammar exercises can be used as a review at the end of the unit or for additional practice.

Problem solving tasks encourage learners to use critical thinking skills and meaningful discussion to find solutions to common problems.

Step Forward offers many different components.

Step-By-Step Lesson Plans

The *Step-By-Step Lesson Plans* provide tips and strategies for conducting *Student Book* activities and applying the lesson to the multilevel classroom.

Multilevel Strategies

For 1C, seat students in mixed-level groups. After the whole-group practice, ask students to take turns reading the sentences aloud. Demonstrate turn-taking, with the first student reading number 1, the second number 2, and so on.

- **Pre-level** Tell students who don't want to read aloud to listen to their classmates and follow along silently.

The *Multilevel Grammar and Literacy Exercises CD-ROM*, a free CD-ROM included with the *Step-By-Step Lesson Plans*, offers additional exercises for pre-level, on-level, and higher-level learners for each grammar point in the *Student Book*. Literacy exercises are also included.

Workbook

The *Workbook* offers additional exercises ideal for independent practice, homework, or review.

Multilevel Activity Book

The *Multilevel Activity Book* features reproducible communication activities to complement the multilevel classroom through a variety of pair, small group, and whole-class activities.

Reproducible student practice pages for literacy-level students include a focus on phonics, sight words, and listening for target sounds.

Literacy Reproducible Book

Audio Program

Audio CDs and Cassettes feature the listening exercises from the *Student Book* as well as conversations, pronunciation, and readings.

Test Generator

The *Test Generator CD-ROM with ExamView® Assessment Suite* offers hundreds of test items for each *Student Book*. Teachers can print out ready-made tests or create their own tests.

Professional Development

Professional Development Task 8

Imagine you want your learners to practice listening carefully during a group task. One behavior you could demonstrate would be leaning forward. Make a list of at least three other behaviors or expressions that careful listeners use.

The *Professional Development Program* offers instructors research-based teaching strategies and activities for single- and multilevel classes, plus Professional Development Tasks like this one.

The First Step

FOCUS ON
- classroom directions
- the alphabet and spelling
- numbers 0–100
- introducing yourself
- talking about the classroom

LESSON 1 The alphabet

1 Learn the alphabet

A Listen and read.

> ## The Alphabet
>
> Aa Bb Cc Dd Ee Ff Gg Hh Ii Jj Kk Ll Mm
> Nn Oo Pp Qq Rr Ss Tt Uu Vv Ww Xx Yy Zz

B Listen again and repeat.

C Listen and look at the pictures.

Listen.

Look.

A.
A.

Repeat.

Point.

Write.

A.

Work with a partner.

Read.

1-2-3.
3 books.

Count.

Spell your name.
R-O-B.

Spell.

☑ Identify letters of the alphabet; spell words

D Listen and point to the letters.

1. a	i	3. g	j	5. p	b	7. y	w
2. i	e	4. h	j	6. m	n	8. f	s

E Work with a partner. Read the letters in 1D.

2 Spell words

A Look at the pictures. Listen and write the letters you hear.

1. b _o_ _o_ k

4. ___ ___ ___ d ___ ___ t

2. p ___ n

5. t e ___ ___ h ___ ___

3. ___ e ___ c ___ ___

6. ___ a p ___ ___

B Listen again and repeat.

**C Work with a partner. Read the words in 2A.
Then spell the words.**

Book.

B-O-O-K.

1 Learn the numbers 0–19

🎧 **A** **Listen and read the numbers.**

0 zero	1 one	2 two	3 three	4 four	5 five	6 six	7 seven

8 eight	9 nine	10 ten	11 eleven	12 twelve	13 thirteen	14 fourteen

15 fifteen	16 sixteen	17 seventeen	18 eighteen	19 nineteen

🎧 **B** **Listen again and repeat.**

C **Work with a partner. Read the numbers in 1A.**

🎧 **D** **Look at the pictures. Listen and repeat the telephone numbers.**

① (562) 555-3217 — (562) 555-3217

② (737) 555-9864 — (737) 555-9864

🎧 **E** **Listen. Write the telephone numbers.**

1. (212) 555 - 4 _2_ _6_ 1
2. (629) 555 - 7 ____ ____ 3
3. (748) 555 - 6 ____ ____ ____
4. (256) 555 - ____ ____ ____ 7

5. (387) 555 - ____ ____ ____ ____
6. (512) 555 - ____ ____ ____ ____
7. (936) 555 - ____ ____ ____ ____
8. (481) 555 - ____ ____ ____ ____

2 Learn the numbers 20–100

A Listen and read the numbers.

20 twenty	21 twenty-one	22 twenty-two	23 twenty-three	24 twenty-four	25 twenty-five
26 twenty-six	27 twenty-seven	28 twenty-eight	29 twenty-nine	30 thirty	40 forty
50 fifty	60 sixty	70 seventy	80 eighty	90 ninety	100 one hundred

B Listen again and repeat.

C Work with a partner. Read the numbers in 2A.

D Listen and repeat.

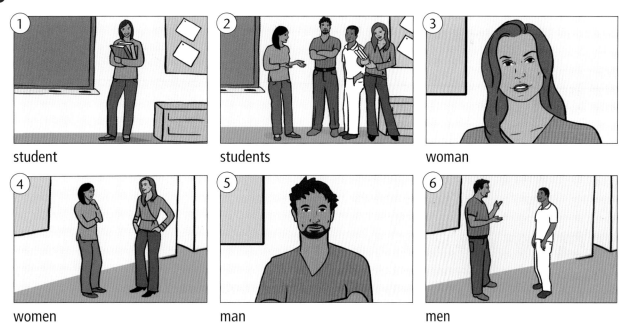

1 student
2 students
3 woman
4 women
5 man
6 men

E Look around your classroom. Count what you see.
Write the numbers.

_____ students

_____ men

_____ women

1 Introduce yourself

A Look at the pictures. Read the conversation.

B Listen and read.

Lorena: Hello. I'm Lorena.
Jin: Excuse me?
Lorena: Lorena. L - O - R - E - N - A.
Jin: Hi. I'm Jin.

C Listen again and repeat.

D Work with your classmates. Practice the conversation.
Use your own information.

A: Hello. I'm _____.

B: Excuse me?

A: _____.

B: Hi. I'm _____.

2 Talk about your classroom

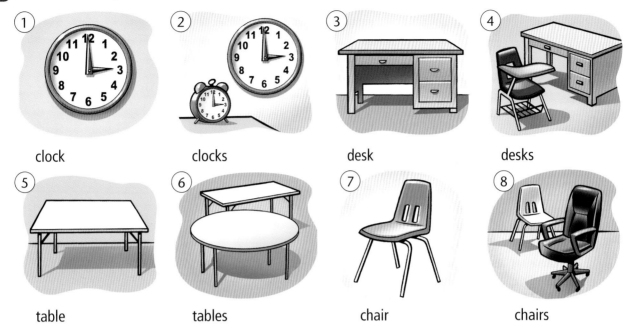

A Look at the pictures. Listen and repeat the words.

1. clock
2. clocks
3. desk
4. desks
5. table
6. tables
7. chair
8. chairs

B Work with a partner. Talk about your classroom.

2 tables

1 clock

C Work with your classmates. Write about your classroom.
Make a list.

    1   clock
    2   desks
    10 tables
    35 students

UNIT **1**

Nice to Meet You

FOCUS ON
- classroom directions
- personal information
- subject pronouns; the verb *be*
- meeting new people
- reading a checklist

LESSON **1** Vocabulary

1 Learn classroom directions

A Look at the pictures. Point to the student.

B Listen and point to the pictures.

C Listen and repeat the words.

1. open
2. close
3. circle
4. say
5. check
6. sign

D Read the new words with a partner.

2 Talk about classroom directions

A Look at the picture. Complete the words.

1. s _a_ y

2. c l o ____ e

3. ____ i r c l e

4. c h ____ c k

5. s ____ g n

6. o p e ____

B Listen and check (✔) what you hear.

1. ____ a. Open your book.   ✔ b. Close your book.

2. ____ a. Circle the pencil.   ____ b. Say *pencil*.

3. ____ a. Sign your name.   ____ b. Say your name.

4. ____ a. Read number one.   ____ b. Check number one.

5. ____ a. Circle your name.   ____ b. Sign your name.

C Listen and follow the directions.

1. Circle the pen.

2. Say *pen*.

3. Close your book.

4. Open your book.

5. Sign your name. _____

TEST YOURSELF ✔

Close your book. Write 3 classroom directions.
Check your spelling in a dictionary.

1 Read about personal information

A Look at the ID card. Say the numbers you see.

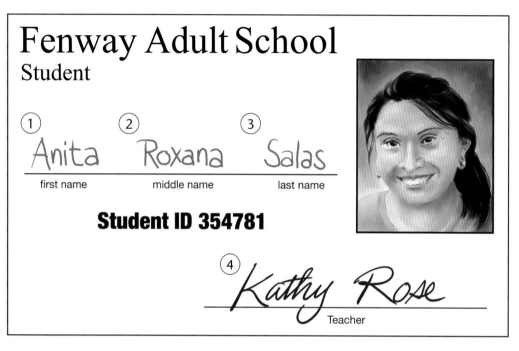

Fenway Adult School
Student

① Anita   ② Roxana   ③ Salas
   first name   middle name   last name

Student ID 354781

④ Kathy Rose
   Teacher

B Listen and repeat the words.

1. first name   3. last name
2. middle name   4. signature

C Listen and read Anita's story.

1. My first name is Anita.   3. I am a student.
2. My last name is Salas.   4. My teacher is Kathy Rose.

D Listen to Alan's story. Circle the correct word.

1. My ____ name is Alan.   (first)   last

2. My ____ name is Woo.   first   last

3. I am a ____ .   student   signature

4. My ____ is Marsha Lee.   teacher   student

Alan

2 Write about yourself

A Write about yourself. Complete the sentences.
Use your own information.

My first name is _____.

My last name is _____.

I am a student.

My teacher is _____.

B Read your story to a partner.

3 Listen for personal information

A Listen and point to the names.

John Wong   Mrs. Boatman   John Wong

B Listen and repeat.

Mrs. Boatman: What is your first name?	**Mrs. Boatman:** What is your last name?
John Wong: John.	**John Wong:** Wong.

C Work with a partner. Practice the conversation in 3B.
Use your own information.

> **TEST YOURSELF** ✓
>
> Copy the sentences. Close your book. Then complete the sentences.
>
> *My first name is _____. My last name is _____.*

1 Learn subject pronouns

A Look at the pictures. Read the words.

1. I
2. he
3. she
4. it
5. they
6. they
7. we

B Look at the words in 1A. Listen and repeat.

C Look at the pictures. Circle *a* or *b*.

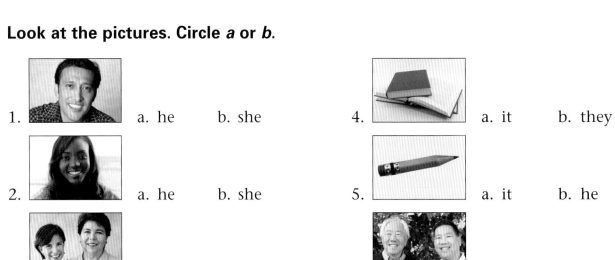

1. a. he   b. she
2. a. he   b. she
3. a. she   b. they
4. a. it   b. they
5. a. it   b. he
6. a. he   b. they

2 Learn the verb *be*

A Look at the pictures. Listen and repeat.

I am a student.

She is a student.

He is a student.

It is a book.

They are students.

We are students.

You are a student.

B Match the parts of the sentence.

  _c_ 1. I   a. is a teacher.

_____ 2. They   b. are students.

_____ 3. It   c. am a student.

_____ 4. She   d. is a pencil.

C Complete the sentences. Use *am*, *is*, or *are*.

1. I _____am_____ a student.

2. He _____ a student.

3. They _____ teachers.

4. It _____ a pen.

5. She _____ Anna.

6. We _____ students.

D Work with a partner. Talk about your classroom.

She is a student. They are tables. It is a pencil.

TEST YOURSELF ✔

Write sentences about your classroom. Compare your sentences with a partner.

He is a student. It is a book.

1 Learn how to meet new people

A Look at the pictures. Read the conversation.

B Listen and read.

Marta: Hi. I am Marta. What is your name?
Trang: My name is Trang.
Marta: Nice to meet you.
Trang: Nice to meet you, too.

C Listen again and repeat.

D Work with your classmates. Practice the conversation.
Use your own information.

A: Hi. I am _____. What is your name?

B: My name is _____.

A: Nice to meet you.

B: Nice to meet you, too.

✔ Use appropriate language for interpersonal communication

2 Listen for spelling

A Listen. Circle *a* or *b*.

1. a. Mary   b. Mark
2. a. John   b. Joan
3. a. Mel   b. Mal
4. a. Sandy   b. Sandi
5. a. Gerry   b. Jerry
6. a. Corbin   b. Corvin

B Listen again and check your answers.

3 Practice your pronunciation

A Listen for *i* and *e* sounds.

i	e
1. nice	5. meet
2. write	6. read
3. five	7. repeat
4. sign	8. please

B Listen and check (✔) the sounds you hear.

	i	e
1.		✔
2.		
3.		
4.		

C Listen again and repeat.

TEST YOURSELF ✓

Copy the conversation. Close your book. Then add your own
information and practice with a partner.

A: Hi. I am _____. What is your name?
B: My name is _____.

---

1 Learn *a* and *an*

A Look at the pictures. Listen and repeat.

a binder

a notebook

an eraser

an English dictionary

B Listen. Write *a* or *an*.

1. _a_ notebook

2. ____ eraser

3. ____ binder

4. ____ English dictionary

5. ____ pen

6. ____ open book

7. ____ English class

8. ____ teacher

2 Get ready to read

A Look at the pictures. Read the words.

adult school

bring

supplies

pages

B Check (✔) the supplies you bring to school.

☐ a pencil   ☐ a binder

☐ a pen   ☐ an English dictionary

☐ an eraser

3 Read a class supplies list

A Read the list.

ABC ADULT SCHOOL

Please bring these supplies to class!

☑ two pencils   ☑ a binder
☑ a pen   ☐ a notebook (100 pages)
☑ an eraser   ☑ paper
☐ an English dictionary

B Look at the list. Circle *yes* or *no*.

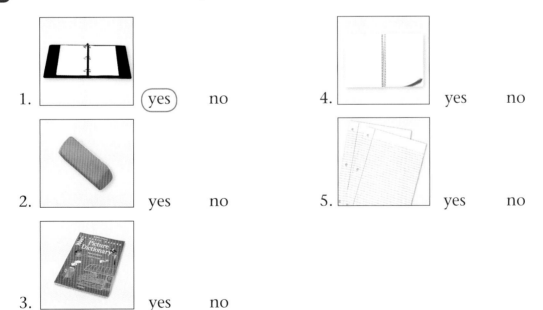

1.   (yes)   no   4.   yes   no

2.   yes   no   5.   yes   no

3.   yes   no

BRING IT TO LIFE

Make a list of supplies for English class.
Bring the list and the supplies to class.

Supplies
paper
2 pens
2 binders

1 Grammar

A Complete the sentences. Use the words in the box.

| She   They   ~~I~~   It |

1. _____I_____ am Tony.

2. _____ are in my class.

3. _____ is my dictionary.

4. _____ is my teacher.

B Complete the sentences. Use *am*, *is*, or *are*.

1. He ___is___ a teacher.

2. She _____ a student.

3. They _____ students.

4. I _____ a student.

5. It _____ an English dictionary.

6. Sam _____ a student.

7. Ali and Chris _____ students.

8. Petra _____ a student.

9. They _____ books.

10. It _____ a notebook.

2 Group work

A Work with 2–3 classmates. Look at the picture. Say what you see.

B Work with your group. Look at the picture in 2A again.
Write what you see. Check your spelling in a dictionary.

1. _____paper_____   4. _____

2. _____   5. _____

3. _____   6. _____

C Work with your classmates. Make a list of the words from 2B.

PROBLEM SOLVING

A Listen. Look at the pictures.

Amaya's Problem

B Work with your classmates. Help Amaya.

a. Ask a student.   b.   Ask the teacher.

How are you feeling?

FOCUS ON
- feelings
- personal information
- negative statements with *be*
- asking about feelings
- reading an envelope

LESSON 1 Vocabulary

1 Learn feeling words

A Look at the pictures. Say what you see.

🎧 **B** Listen and point to the pictures.

🎧 **C** Listen and repeat the words.

1. fine	4. sad	7. tired
2. happy	5. hungry	8. sick
3. excited	6. thirsty	

D Read the new words with a partner.

2 Talk about feelings

A **Look at the picture. Complete the words.**

1. e x _c_ i t e d

2. s ___ d

3. ___ i n ___

4. t i r ___ d

5. h a p ___ y

6. t h i r s ___ y

7. ___ u n g r y

8. ___ i c k

B **Listen and repeat.**

1. **Zita:** I am tired.
   Inez: I am tired, too.

2. **Al:** I am hungry.
   Lam: I am thirsty.

C **Work with a partner. Practice the conversations. Use your own ideas.**

1. A: I am _____.

   B: I am _____, too.

2. A: I am _____.

   B: I am _____.

TEST YOURSELF ✔

Close your book. Write 3 words for feelings. Check your spelling in a dictionary.

1 Read about personal information

A Look at the form. Point to the first name.

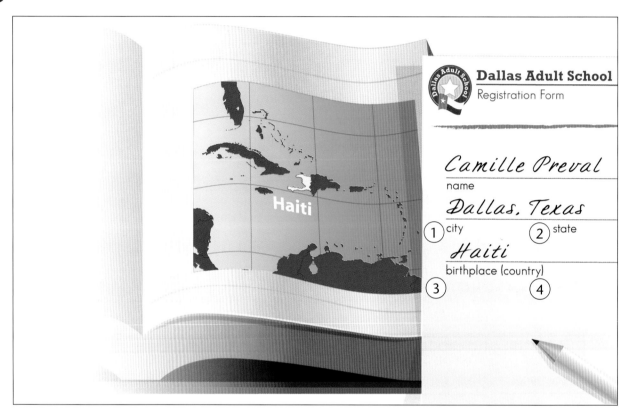

🎧 **B** Listen and repeat the words.

1. city
2. state
3. birthplace
4. country

🎧 **C** Listen and read Camille's story.

1. My name is Camille.
2. I am from Haiti.
3. Now I am in Dallas, Texas.
4. I am happy in Dallas.

D Look at 1C. Write about Camille.

1. name _____Camille_____

2. birthplace _____

3. city _____, state _____

Camille

2 Write about personal information

A Write about personal information. Complete the sentences. Use your own information.

My name is _____.

I am from _____.

Now I am in _____, _____.

B Read your story to a partner.

3 Listen for countries

A Listen and point to the countries you hear.

China

Vietnam

B Listen and repeat.

A: Where are you from?   A: Where is Lian from?
B: I am from Vietnam.   B: She is from China.

C Work with a partner. Practice the conversation in 3B. Use your own ideas.

┌─ TEST YOURSELF ✔ ─────────────────────────────────
│
│ Copy the sentences. Close your book. Then complete the sentences.
│ Use your own ideas.
│   *I am from _____. _____ is from _____.*
│
└──

1 Learn negative statements with *be*

A Look at the pictures. Read the sentences.

He is not sad. He is happy.

She is not sick. She is tired.

B Study the chart. Listen and repeat.

I	am		
You	are		
He She It	is	not	tired.
We They	are		

C Complete the sentences. Circle *a* or *b*. Then read the sentences with a partner.

1. I ____ tired.

   a. is not   (b.) am not

2. She ____ tired.

   a. is not   b. am not

3. We ____ tired.

   a. is not   b. are not

4. They ____ tired.

   a. is not   b. are not

D Complete the sentences. Use *am not, is not,* or *are not*.

1. She _____is not_____ excited.

2. He _____ happy.

3. They _____ hungry.

4. I _____ sad.

5. You _____ sick.

6. We _____ thirsty.

✔ Use negative statements and contractions with *be* to express feelings

2 Learn contractions with *be*

A Look at the pictures. Listen and read the sentences.

I'm not from Texas.
I'm from Mexico.

She's not tired.
She's excited.

He's not happy.
He's sick.

They're not in California.
They're in Colorado.

It's not a city.
It's a state.

You're not a student.
You're a teacher.

We're not teachers.
We're students.

B Match the sentences.

_c_ 1. I am not sad.   a. She's tired.

____ 2. She is not tired.   b. They're happy.

____ 3. She is tired.   c. I'm not sad.

____ 4. It is not a state.   d. They're not happy.

____ 5. They are happy.   e. She's not tired.

____ 6. They are not happy.   f. It's not a state.

C Write new sentences. Use contractions.

1. She is not excited. _____She's not excited._____

2. He is not a student. _____

3. We are not sick. _____

D Work with a partner. Read the sentences in 2C.

TEST YOURSELF ✔

Write sentences about feelings. Use contractions. Compare your sentences with a partner.

I'm tired. They're not happy.

1 Learn to ask about feelings

A Look at the pictures. Read the conversation.

B Listen and read.

Pedro: How are you feeling?
Vanna: I'm fine. How are you feeling?
Pedro: I'm sick.
Vanna: Oh, I'm sorry.

C Listen again and repeat.

D Work with a partner. Practice the conversation. Use your own ideas.

A: How are you feeling?
B: I'm _____.
   How are you feeling?
A: I'm _____.
B: Oh, I'm sorry.

Need help?

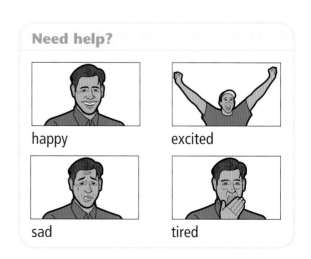

happy   excited

sad   tired

2 Listen for personal information

A Listen. Circle *a* or *b*.

1. a. How are you feeling?   b. Where are you from?
2. a. Where are you from?   b. What's your name?
3. a. How are you feeling?   b. What's your name?

B Listen and answer the questions. Circle *a* or *b*.

1. (a.) I'm happy.   b. My name is Pao.
2. a. I'm from China.   b. My name is Leila.
3. a. I'm tired.   b. I'm from China.
4. a. My name is Luis.   b. I'm from Mexico.

3 Practice your pronunciation

A Listen and count the syllables (•).

1 syllable	2 syllables	3 syllables
fine	hap py	ex cit ed
•	• •	• • •

B Listen and check (✔) the correct boxes.

	1. fine	2. thirsty	3. telephone	4. hungry	5. sad	6. signature
1 syllable	✔					
2 syllables						
3 syllables						

C Listen again and check your answers. Then repeat the words.

TEST YOURSELF ✔

Copy the conversation. Close your book. Then add your
own ideas and practice with a partner.

A: *How are you feeling?*
B: *I'm _____.*

Unit 2 Lesson 4   **27**

1 Learn about addresses

A Look at the picture. Listen and repeat.

1. address
2. zip code

B Match.

_c_ 1. address   a. 92110

____ 2. state   b. California

____ 3. zip code   c. 2091 Oak Street, San Diego, California 92110

____ 4. city   d. San Diego

2 Get ready to read

A Look at the pictures. Read the words.

Need help?

GA = Georgia
NC = North Carolina

1. envelope
2. return address
3. mailing address
4. form

River City Adult School
Student Information

David   Brown
first name   last name

16   Spring Street
number   street

Helen,   GA   74112
city   state   zip code

B Complete the form. Use your own information.

number	street
city	state zip code

3 Read a form and an envelope

A Read the form and the envelope.

River City Adult School

Student Information

Susan   Kirkwood
first name   last name

609   First Street
number   street

Atlanta,   GA   74354
city   state   zip code

Susan Kirkwood
609 First Street
Atlanta, GA 74354

      River City Adult School
      3712 Maple Street
      Salem, NC 60611

B Look at the form and envelope. Circle *a* or *b*.

1. Susan is in ____.

   (a.) Atlanta   b. Salem

2. River City Adult School is in ____.

   a. Atlanta   b. Salem

3. The address of the school is ____.

   a. 609 First Street   b. 3712 Maple Street

4. Susan's zip code is ____.

   a. 609   b. 74354

BRING IT TO LIFE

Bring an envelope to class. Circle the mailing address.
Check (✔) the return address.

1 Grammar

A Complete the sentences. Use contractions.

1. It ___'s not___ a book. It ___'s___ a pencil.

2. She _____ sad. She _____ happy.

3. They _____ sick. They _____ tired.

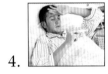

4. He _____ happy. He _____ sick.

(707)
555-1428

5. It _____ a zip code. It _____ a phone number.

2 Group work

A Work with 2–3 classmates. Look at the picture. Say what you see.

B Work with your group. Look at the picture in 2A again.
Write what you see. Check your spelling in a dictionary.

1. _____happy_____   4. _____

2. _____   5. _____

3. _____   6. _____

C Work with your classmates. Make a list of the words from 2B.

PROBLEM SOLVING

A Listen. Look at the pictures.

Gary's Problem

B Work with your classmates. Help Gary.

a. Go to the post office. Ask
   for help.

b. Look on the computer.

UNIT **3**

What time is it?

FOCUS ON
- telling time
- places in the community
- *Yes/No* questions with *be*
- asking about time
- reading a bus schedule

LESSON **1**   Vocabulary

1 Learn to tell time

A Look at the pictures. Count the clocks.

🎧 **B** Listen and point to the pictures.

🎧 **C** Listen and repeat the words.

1. morning	4. night	7. 2:30	10. midnight
2. afternoon	5. 2:00	8. 2:45	
3. evening	6. 2:15	9. noon	

D Read the new words with a partner.

2 Talk about time

A Look at the pictures. Complete the words.

1. m __o__ __r__ n i n g

2. n ____ o n

3. a ____ t e r n o o n

4. e ____ e n i n g

5. n i g ____ t

6. m i d n ____ g h t

B Listen and repeat.

A: What time is it?

B: It's 6:30.

C Work with a partner. Point to the clocks in 1B and 2A. Practice the conversation.

A: What time is it?

B: It's _____.

TEST YOURSELF ✔

Close your book. Write 3 times of day. Check your spelling in a dictionary.

1 Read about places in the community

A Look at the pictures. Say the times.

8:00   Cindy   9:30   10:00   10:30

1:30   4:00   6:00

B Listen and repeat the words.

1. go to the store
2. go to the library
3. go to school
4. go to English class
5. go to work
6. go to the clinic
7. go home

C Listen and read Cindy's story.

1. I go to the store at 8:00.
2. I go to the library at 9:30.
3. I go to school at 10:00.
4. I go to English class at 10:30.

🎧 **D** Listen to Rick's story. Circle the correct word.

1. I go to ____ at 9:00.   ⟨school⟩   the store

2. I go to ____ at 1:00.   the clinic   the library

3. I go to English ____ at 2:30.   class   the clinic

4. I go to ____ at 6:00.   home   work

Rick

2 Write about your day

A Write about your day. Complete the sentences. Use your own ideas.

I go to _____ at _____.

I go to _____ at _____.

I go to English class at _____.

B Read your story to a partner.

3 Listen for *a.m.* and *p.m.*

A Look at the pictures. Read the times and sentences.

8 a.m. = 8:00 in the morning
I go to work at 8 a.m.

8 p.m. = 8:00 in the evening
I go home at 8 p.m.

🎧 **B** Listen. Circle *morning* or *evening*.

1. ⟨morning⟩   evening   3. morning   evening
2. morning   evening   4. morning   evening

🎧 **C** Listen again. Write the times you hear.

1. __7 a.m.__   2. _____   3. _____   4. _____

TEST YOURSELF ✔

Copy the sentences. Close your book. Then complete the sentences.
Use your own ideas.

I go to _____ at _____ in the morning. I go _____ at _____ .

1 Learn *Yes/No* questions with *be*

A Look at the pictures. Read the questions.

Are you at school?

Is it 6:00?

Is he at the clinic?

B Study the chart. Listen and repeat.

	he she	at school?
Is		
	it	6:00?
Are	you they	at home?

C Complete the questions. Use *Is* or *Are*. Then read the questions with a partner.

1. ___Is___ he at school?

2. _____ she at school?

3. _____ it 6:00?

4. _____ you at home?

5. _____ they at home?

D Complete the statements and questions. Use *?* or *.*

1. She's at the clinic __.__

2. Are you at work ____

3. Is it 5:00 ____

4. He's at the library ____

5. It's closed ____

6. She's at home ____

7. Is he at the clinic ____

8. They're at the store ____

✔ Use *Yes/No* questions and short answers with *be* to talk about time and location

2 Learn short answers with *be*

A Listen. Repeat the questions and answers.

1

A: Are you at the store?
B: Yes, I am.
B: Are you at work?
A: No, I'm not.

2

A: Is she at work?
B: Yes, she is.
A: Is she at the clinic?
B: No, she's not.

3

A: Is he at school?
B: Yes, he is.
A: Is he at the library?
B: No, he's not.

4

A: Is it 10 a.m.?
B: Yes, it is.
A: Is it 10 p.m.?
B: No, it's not.

5

A: Are they at the library?
B: Yes, they are.
A: Are they at home?
B: No, they're not.

6

A: Are we happy?
B: Yes, we are.
A: Are we hungry?
B: No, we're not.

B Read the questions. Complete the answers. Use short answers with *be*.

1. A: Is it 4 p.m.?

   B: No, it 's not_____.

2. A: Is she at the store?

   B: Yes, she _____.

3. A: Are you at school?

   B: Yes, I _____.

4. A: Are they at the store?

   B: No, they _____.

C Work with a partner. Ask the questions. Answer with *Yes, I am.* or *No, I'm not.*

1. Are you at school?
2. Are you at the library?
3. Are you a student?
4. Are you a teacher?

5. Are you at home?
6. Are you in English class?
7. Are you from Mexico?
8. Are you from China?

TEST YOURSELF ✔

Write *Yes/No* questions and short answers with *be*.
Compare your sentences with a partner.

Are you at the library? No, I'm not.

1 Learn to ask about time

A Look at the pictures. Read the conversation.

B Listen and read.

Alfredo: Excuse me. What time is it?
Pilar: It's 8:00.
Alfredo: Is the store open?
Pilar: No, it's not.

C Listen again and repeat.

D Work with a partner. Practice the conversation. Use your own ideas.

A: Excuse me. What time is it?

B: It's _____.

A: Is the _____ open?

B: No, it's not.

Need help?

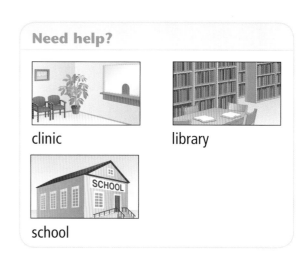

clinic   library

school

✔ Use appropriate language to ask for information about places in the community

2 Listen for times

Listen and point to the pictures.

Listen again. What times do you hear? Circle _a_ or _b_.

1. a. 10 a.m.   b. 10 p.m.

2. a. 8:00 in the morning   b. 8:00 in the evening

3. a. 9 a.m.   b. 9 p.m.

4. a. 10:00 in the morning   b. 10:00 in the evening

3 Practice your pronunciation

Listen to the questions.

1. Is the store open?   2. Are you at the office?

Listen and repeat the questions.

1. Is it 4:00?   5. Are they happy?
2. Is Daniel at the store?   6. Is he at the clinic?
3. Is the class in the morning?   7. Are they at work?
4. Are you at home?   8. Are you hungry?

C **Work with a partner. Read the questions in 3B.**

TEST YOURSELF ✔

Copy the conversation. Close your book. Then add your
own ideas and practice with a partner.

A: Is the _____ open?
B: _____.

Unit 3 Lesson 4 **39**

1 Learn about kinds of transportation

A Look at the pictures. Listen and repeat.

bus   car   plane   train

B Listen. Circle *a* or *b*.

1. a.   b.   3. a.   b.

2. a.   b.   4. a.   b.

2 Get ready to read

A Look at the pictures. Read the words.

hour

minute

	207	209	621	613	121
Hill	5:00		7:00	8:00	8:15
Glen		6:00	7:15		8:45
Elm	5:20	6:25	7:45	8:20	9:00
Vail		6:30	8:00		9:15
Oak	5:30	6:45	8:15	8:30	9:30

schedule

A: How long is the trip?
B: It's one hour and 30 minutes.

B Work with your classmates. How long is your English class?

3 Read a bus schedule

A Read the bus schedule.

Bus Number	Newport	Springfield	Salem	Sundale
23	7:00 a.m.	——	10:00 a.m.	10:30 a.m.
61	7:30 a.m.	9:00 a.m.	10:50 a.m.	11:20 a.m.
94	9:30 a.m.	11:00 a.m.	——	1:10 p.m.
57	4:00 p.m.	——	7:00 p.m.	7:30 p.m.

B Look at the schedule. Circle *yes* or *no*.

1. Bus 94 is at Springfield. Is it 10:00 a.m.?   yes   (no)

2. Bus 61 is at Newport. Is it 7:30 a.m.?   yes   no

3. Bus 23 is at Sundale. Is it 10:30 a.m.?   yes   no

4. Bus 57 is at Salem. Is it 7:30 p.m.?   yes   no

C Look at the schedule. Answer the questions for Carlos. Circle *a* or *b*.

1. How long is the trip to Sundale on Bus 23?

   a. 2 hours and 30 minutes

   b. 3 hours and 30 minutes

2. How long is the trip to Sundale on Bus 61?

   a. 3 hours and 30 minutes

   b. 3 hours and 50 minutes

3. How long is the trip to Sundale on Bus 94?

   a. 2 hours and 40 minutes

   b. 3 hours and 40 minutes

Carlos is in Newport.

BRING IT TO LIFE

Bring a bus or train schedule to class.
Circle 1 new word.

1 Grammar

A Read the questions. Complete the answers.

1. **A:** Is Deenah at the store?

   B: No, _____ she's not _____.

2. **A:** Is Monica at the clinic?

   B: Yes, _____.

3. **A:** Is Bob at home?

   B: Yes, _____.

4. **A:** Are the students at the library?

   B: Yes, _____.

5. **A:** Is it 11:00?

   B: No, _____.

6. **A:** Is he at work?

   B: No, _____.

7. **A:** Is she at home?

   B: No, _____.

2 Group work

A Work with 2–3 classmates. Look at the pictures. Say what you see.

B Work with your group. Look at the pictures in 2A again. Write what you see. Check your spelling in a dictionary.

1. _____ *clinic* _____   4. _____

2. _____   5. _____

3. _____   6. _____

C Work with your classmates. Make a list of the words from 2B.

PROBLEM SOLVING

A Listen. Look at the pictures.

Tony's Problem

B Work with your classmates. Help Tony.

a. Leave class early.   b. Go to class late.

UNIT 4

What day is it?

FOCUS ON
- days
- months
- *on* and *at*; information questions
- saying goodbye
- ordinal numbers

LESSON 1 Vocabulary

1 Learn the days of the week

A Look at the calendar. What time is English class?

B Listen and point to the days.

Sunday	Monday	Tuesday	Wednesday	Thursday	Friday	Saturday
①	②	③	④	⑤	⑥	⑦
		9:00 – 12:00 English class	3:00 clinic			
	1	2	3	4	5	6
⑧						⑨

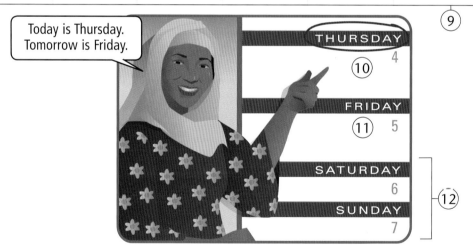

Today is Thursday.
Tomorrow is Friday.

THURSDAY 4 ⑩

FRIDAY 5 ⑪

SATURDAY 6

SUNDAY 7

⑫

C Listen and repeat the words.

1. Sunday
2. Monday
3. Tuesday
4. Wednesday
5. Thursday
6. Friday
7. Saturday
8. day
9. week
10. today
11. tomorrow
12. weekend

D Read the new words with a partner.

2 Talk about the days of the week

A Look at the picture. Complete the words.

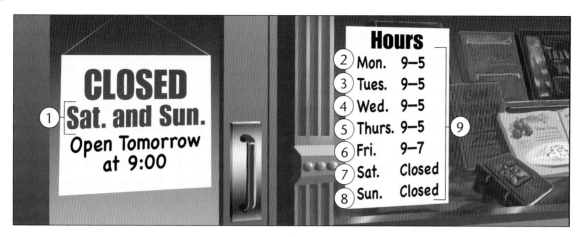

1. w e e __k__ e n d

2. M ____ n d a y

3. T u e s ____ a y

4. ____ e d n e s d a y

5. T h ____ r s d a y

6. F r i d a ____

7. S a t u ____ d a y

8. S u n d ____ y

9. w e ____ k

B Listen and repeat.

A: What day is it?

B: It's Thursday.

C Work with a partner. Point to the days in 2A.
Practice the conversation.

A: What day is it?

B: It's _____.

TEST YOURSELF ✔

Close your book. Write 3 days of the week. Check your spelling in a dictionary.

1 Read about the months

A Look at the picture. Point to the number 24.

B Listen and repeat the words.

1. January
2. February
3. March
4. April
5. May
6. June
7. July
8. August
9. September
10. October
11. November
12. December
13. month
14. year

C Listen and read Olga's story.

1. It's October.
2. Next month is November.
3. My birthday is in November.

🎧 **D** Listen to Bill's story. Circle the correct word.

1. It's ____. (April) August

2. Next month is ____. March May

3. My birthday is in ____. June July

Bill

2 Write about the months

A Write about the months. Complete the sentences. Use your own information.

It's _____.

Next month is _____.

My birthday is in _____.

B Read your story to a partner.

3 Listen for years

🎧 **A** Listen and repeat the years.

1. 1948   5. 1986
2. 1952   6. 2000
3. 1963   7. 2008
4. 1975   8. 2011

🎧 **B** Listen. Circle *a* or *b*.

1. a. 1964   (b.) 1946
2. a. 2007   b. 2008
3. a. 1985   b. 1958
4. a. 1972   b. 1992
5. a. March   b. May
6. a. February 1956 b. February 1965

TEST YOURSELF ✔

Copy the sentences. Close your book. Then complete the sentences.

It's _____. *It's* _____.
     day   month

1 Learn *on* with days and *at* with times

A **Look at the picture.**
Read the sentences.

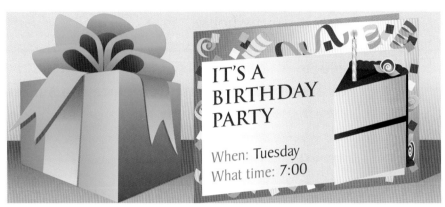

IT'S A
BIRTHDAY
PARTY

When: Tuesday
What time: 7:00

The party is on Tuesday. The party is at 7:00.

B **Study the chart. Listen and repeat.**

The birthday party is	on	Tuesday	at	7:00.
The class party is		Thursday		5:00.

C **Complete the sentences. Circle *on* or *at*.**
Then read the sentences with a partner.

1. The birthday party is ____ Tuesday.

   (on)   at

2. The birthday party is ____ 7:00.

   on   at

3. The class party is ____ 5:00.

   on   at

4. The class party is ____ Thursday.

   on   at

D **Listen. Circle *on* or *at*.**

1. (on)   at   5. on   at
2. on   at   6. on   at
3. on   at   7. on   at
4. on   at   8. on   at

2 Learn information questions

🎧 **A** **Listen. What time is the party?**

Abena: <u>When</u> is the birthday party?
Gloria: It's on Tuesday.
Abena: <u>Where</u> is the party?
Gloria: It's at my house.
Abena: <u>What</u> time is the party?
Gloria: It's at 6:00.
Abena: Are you excited?
Gloria: Yes, I am!

🎧 **B** **Listen again. Complete the questions.**

1. **Abena:** _____ is the birthday party?

   Gloria: It's on Tuesday.

2. **Abena:** _____ is the party?

   Gloria: It's at my house.

3. **Abena:** _____ time is the party?

   Gloria: It's at 6:00.

C **Read the invitation. Answer the questions. Circle a or b.**

1. When is the party?

   (a.) It's on Thursday.   b. It's at Pizza Town.

2. What time is the party?

   a. It's on Thursday.   b. It's at 6:00.

3. Where is the party?

   a. Yes, it is.   b. It's at Pizza Town.

4. Is the party on Thursday?

   a. Yes, it is.   b. It's at Pizza Town.

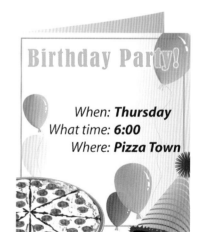

D **Work with a partner. Read the questions and answers in 2C.**

TEST YOURSELF ✔

Write sentences for a party invitation. Compare your sentences with a partner.

The party is on Friday. It's at 4:30.

1 Learn to say goodbye

A Look at the pictures. Read the conversations.

B Listen and read.

Arun: Goodbye. Have a nice weekend.
Oscar: Thanks. You, too. See you Monday.

Mrs. Robledo: Bye. Have a nice evening.
Tuan: Thanks. You, too. See you tomorrow.

C Listen again and repeat.

D Work with your classmates. Practice the conversation. Use your own ideas.

A: Goodbye. Have a nice _____.

B: Thanks. You, too. See you _____.

✔ Use appropriate language to say goodbye

2 Listen for dates with years

A Read the dates.

June 4, 2009 = 6/4/2009
April 6, 2009 = 4/6/2009
July 12, 1960 = 7/12/1960
December 7, 1960 = 12/7/1960

B Listen. Circle *a* or *b*.

1. a. 6/4/1999   (b.) 4/6/1999   5. a. 2/1/2007   b. 1/2/2007

2. a. 7/12/1960   b. 12/7/1960   6. a. 3/5/1951   b. 5/3/1951

3. a. 11/9/1982   b. 9/11/1982   7. a. 11/5/1974   b. 5/11/1974

4. a. 8/10/2009   b. 10/8/2009   8. a. 1/8/2008   b. 8/1/2008

C Work with a partner. Look at the dates in 2B. Say the months.

3 Practice your pronunciation

A Listen to the pronunciation of *t* and *th*.

See you tomorrow.   Thanks. See you Thursday.

B Listen and repeat the words.

t	*th*
1. tomorrow	4. Thursday
2. Tuesday	5. thirsty
3. tired	6. thanks

C Listen. Check (✔) the sounds you hear.

	1.	2.	3.	4.	5.	6.
t	✔					
th						

TEST YOURSELF ✔

Copy the conversation. Close your book. Then add your
own ideas and practice with a partner.

A: Goodbye. _____ .
B: _____ .

1 Learn about ordinal numbers

🎧 **A** Look at the calendar. Listen and point to the dates.

March

Sun.	Mon.	Tues.	Wed.	Thurs.	Fri.	Sat.
1 first	2 second	3 third	4 fourth	5 fifth	6 sixth	7 seventh
8 eighth	9 ninth	10 tenth	11 eleventh	12 twelfth	13 thirteenth	14 fourteenth
15 fifteenth	16 sixteenth	17 seventeenth	18 eighteenth	19 nineteenth	20 twentieth	21 twenty-first
22 twenty-second	23 twenty-third	24 twenty-fourth	25 twenty-fifth	26 twenty-sixth	27 twenty-seventh	28 twenty-eighth
29 twenty-ninth	30 thirtieth	31 thirty-first				

🎧 **B** Listen again and repeat.

C Match the numbers with the ordinals.

_c_ 1. one   a. second

____ 2. two   b. fourth

____ 3. three   c. first

____ 4. four   d. fifth

____ 5. five   e. third

2 Get ready to read

A Look at the pictures. Read the words.

winter break

registration

the last day of school

B Work with your classmates. Complete the sentences.

1. The last day of school is _____.

2. Winter break is from _____ to _____.

3 Read a school calendar

A Read the school calendar.

Valley Adult School Calendar

Important Dates

September 5-9 .... registration

September 12 .... the first day of school

November 24-25 .... Thanksgiving holiday

December 20-January 3 .... winter break

June 20 .... the last day of school

B Look at the calendar. Circle *a* or *b*.

1. ____ is September 5–9.

   a. Winter break   (b.) Registration

2. ____ is December 20–January 3.

   a. The first day of school   b. Winter break

3. The ____ day of school is June 20.

   a. first   b. last

4. The ____ day of school is September 12.

   a. first   b. last

BRING IT TO LIFE

Find the calendar for your school. Bring it to class.
Circle 2 new words.

May Calendar

Computer lab............. 5/3

Language lab 5/8

Mother's Day 5/13

Memorial Day 5/28

1 Grammar

A **Complete the questions. Circle _a_ or _b_.**

1. **A:** ____ is your birthday?
    B: It's on April 25.
    a. Where
    (b.) When

2. **A:** ____ time is the party?
    B: It's at 6:00.
    a. What
    b. When

3. **A:** ____ is the party?
    B: It's at my house.
    a. Where
    b. What

4. **A:** ____ the party on Thursday?
    B: Yes, it is.
    a. Is
    b. When

5. **A:** ____ is the first day of school?
    B: September 10.
    a. Where
    b. When

6. **A:** ____ you happy?
    B: Yes, I am.
    a. Are
    b. Where

B **Complete the sentences. Use _on_ or _at_.**

1. Registration is _____on_____ Thursday.

2. I go to work _____ 6:00.

3. I go to the library _____ Mondays.

4. The party is _____ December 2 _____ 7:00.

2 Group work

A **Work with 2–3 classmates. Look at the picture. Say what you see.**

B Work with your group. Look at the picture in 2A again.
Write what you see. Check your spelling in a dictionary.

1. _____month_____   4. _____

2. _____   5. _____

3. _____   6. _____

C Work with your classmates. Make a list of the words from 2B.

PROBLEM SOLVING

A Listen. Look at the pictures.

Sharon's Problem

B Work with your classmates. Help Sharon.

a. Call the school.

b. Go to school now.

How much is it?

FOCUS ON
- money
- shopping
- *This*, *That*, *These*, and *Those*
- asking about prices
- reading a check

LESSON **1**   Vocabulary

1 Learn words for money

A Look at the pictures. Say the numbers.

B Listen and point to the pictures.

41¢

1¢ = $0.01

5¢ = $0.05

10¢ = $0.10

25¢ = $0.25

C Listen and repeat the words.

1. bills	4. cents	7. dime
2. dollar	5. penny	8. quarter
3. coins	6. nickel	

D Read the new words with a partner.

2 Talk about money

A Look at the picture. Complete the words.

1. p _e_ _n_ n y

2. d i ___ e

3. b ___ ___ l s

4. ___ o l l ___ r

5. ___ ___ i n s

6. n i c ___ ___ l

7. ___ u a ___ t e r

8. c ___ ___ t s

B Listen and repeat.

1. **A:** How much is it?
   B: It's 25¢.

2. **A:** How much is it?
   B: It's $6.

C Listen. Circle *a* or *b*.

1. a. 65¢   (b.) 75¢
2. a. $2   b. $12
3. a. 35¢   b. 45¢
4. a. $6   b. $16
5. a. $5   b. $7
6. a. 80¢   b. 90¢

D Work with a partner. Point to the money in 2A.
Practice the conversation.

A: How much is it?

B: It's _____.

TEST YOURSELF ✔

Close your book. Write 3 words for money. Check your spelling in a dictionary.

1 Read about shopping

A Look at the picture. Say the numbers.

B Listen and repeat the words.

1. price
2. pants
3. shirt
4. sweater
5. shoes

6. socks
7. clothes
8. cheap
9. expensive

C Listen and read Daniela's story.

1. Clothes Mart is a good store.
2. The clothes are good.
3. The prices are cheap.

D Listen to Ken's story. Circle the correct word.

1. Shoe World is a good ____.   (store)   sock

2. The ____ are good.   sweaters   shoes

3. The ____ are cheap.   shoes   socks

Ken

---

2 Write about shopping

A Write about shopping. Complete the sentences.
Use your own ideas.

_____ is a good store.

The _____ are good.

The _____ are cheap.

B Read your story to a partner.

---

3 Listen for prices

A Listen and repeat.

1. $1.50   4. $12.25
2. $2.30   5. $15.50
3. $5.45   6. $7.60

B Listen and write the prices.

1. $ _3_._2__5_

2. $____.____ ____

3. $____.____ ____

4. $____.____ ____

5. $____.____ ____

6. $____.____ ____

TEST YOURSELF ✔

Copy the sentences. Close your book. Then complete the sentences.

The _____ is cheap. It's $_____.

1 Learn *This* and *That*

🎧 **A** **Look at the pictures. Listen and repeat the sentences.**

This shirt is $35.   That shirt is $42.   This sweater is $22.   That sweater is $54.

B **Look at 1A. Write *This* or *That*.**

1. _____ shirt is $35.

2. _____ shirt is $42.

3. _____ sweater is $22.

4. _____ sweater is $54.

C **Look at the pictures. Circle *a* or *b*. Then read the sentences with a partner.**

1. ___ sweater is $12.
   a.) This   b. That

2. ___ sweater is $9.99.
   a. This   b. That

3. ___ dictionary is $5.99.
   a. This   b. That

4. ___ dictionary is $42.
   a. This   b. That

2 Learn *These* and *Those*

A Look at the pictures. Listen and repeat the sentences.

<u>These</u> pants are $14.

<u>Those</u> pants are $45.

B Match the pictures with the sentences.

__*b*__ 1. These pants are $45.

____ 2. Those pants are $45.

____ 3. These shoes are $34.50.

____ 4. Those shoes are $34.50.

____ 5. These pens are $3.99.

____ 6. Those pens are $3.99.

C Complete the sentences. Circle *a* or *b*.

1. ____ pencil is 25¢.
   a. This   b. These

2. ____ shoes are $30.
   a. That   b. Those

3. ____ clock is expensive.
   a. That   b. Those

4. ____ notebooks are cheap.
   a. This   b. These

D Work with a partner. Read the sentences in 2B and 2C.

TEST YOURSELF ✓

Write sentences using *This*, *That*, *These*, or *Those*. Compare your sentences with a partner.

This shirt is expensive. Those pencils are 30¢.

1 Learn to talk about prices

A Look at the pictures. Read the conversation.

B Listen and read.

George: How much is the shirt?
Kumi: It's $35.
George: How much are the shoes?
Kumi: They're $33.
George: That's cheap!

C Listen again and repeat.

D Work with a partner. Practice the conversation. Use your own ideas.

A: How much is the _____?

B: It's _____.

A: How much are the _____?

B: They're _____.

A: That's _____!

Need help?

How much is the _____?

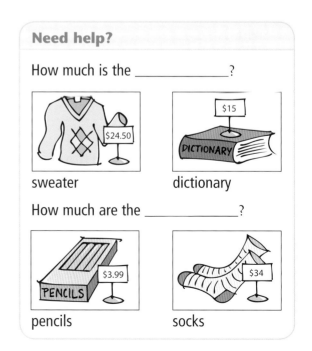

sweater   dictionary

How much are the _____?

pencils   socks

2 Listen for change amounts

A Look at the money. What coins do you see?

B Listen. Circle *a* or *b*.

1. a. b.

2. a. b.

3. a. b.

4. a. b.

5. a. b.

6. a. b.

3 Real-life math

A Look at the picture. Say the prices.

EVERYTHING 50% off

1 Erasers **$0.50** 2 Notebook paper **$1.00** 3 Box of envelopes **$2.50** 4 Small desk lamp **$30.00**

B Do the math. Write the sale price.

1. $0.50 × 0.5 = $___0.25___   An eraser is $___0.25___.
2. $1.00 × 0.5 = $_____   The paper is $_____.
3. $2.50 × 0.5 = $_____   The envelopes are $_____.
4. $30.00 × 0.5 = $_____   A lamp is $_____.

> **TEST YOURSELF** ✓
>
> Copy the conversation. Close your book. Then add your own ideas and practice with a partner.
>
> *A: How much is* _____?
> *B: It's* _____.

1 Learn about ways to pay

A Look at the pictures. Listen and repeat.

pay

cash

check

credit card

debit card

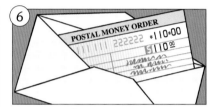
money order

B Listen. Circle *a* or *b*.

1. a.   b.

2. a.   b.

3. a.   b.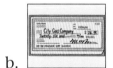

4. a.   b.

2 Get ready to read

A Look at the pictures. Read the words.

① Central Electric Company

Amount Due: $57.32

electric bill

② KANSAS GAS COMPANY

Amount Due: $48.61

gas bill

B Complete the sentences with *expensive* or *cheap*.

1. My gas bill is _____.

2. My electric bill is _____.

3 Read a check

A Read the bill and the check.

Central Electric Company

Amount Due: $56.23

Joel and Ana Marino
4219 Brook Street
Topeka, Kansas 61401   2529

Date _7/12/2009_

PAY TO THE
ORDER OF _Central Electric Company_ $ | 56.23 |

fifty-six and 23/100   DOLLARS

FOR _electric bill_   _Joel Marino_

87255654653   06128745379

B Look at the gas bill. Complete the check.

KANSAS GAS COMPANY

Amount Due: $32.89

State Bank
                                             2530

Date _____

PAY TO THE
ORDER OF _____ $ |_____|

_____   DOLLARS

FOR_____   _____

12345470053   06457820579

BRING IT TO LIFE

Bring a gas bill or an electric bill to class.
Circle 1 new word.

1 Grammar

A Complete the sentences. Use *This* or *These*.

1. ___This___ sweater is expensive.
2. _____ shirts are cheap.
3. _____ lamp is $17.99.
4. _____ pants are $25.

5. _____ notebook is $3.
6. _____ pencils are cheap.
7. _____ envelopes are 30¢.
8. _____ eraser is $1.50.

B Complete the sentences. Use *That* or *Those*.

1. ___That___ book is expensive.
2. _____ sweaters are expensive.
3. _____ lamp is $10.99.
4. _____ shoes are $28.

5. _____ pencil is 10¢.
6. _____ erasers are expensive.
7. _____ envelopes are cheap.
8. _____ dictionary is $16.

C Complete the sentences with *is* or *are*.

1. Those socks __are__ $3.99.
2. This shirt _____ expensive.
3. That book _____ $11.
4. Those clothes _____ cheap.

5. That pen _____ $1.50.
6. These pants _____ $25.
7. That price _____ good.
8. This store _____ expensive.

2 Group work

A Work with 2–3 classmates. Look at the picture. Say what you see.

B Work with your group. Look at the picture in 2A again.
Write what you see. Check your spelling in a dictionary.

1. _____shirt_____   4. _____

2. _____   5. _____

3. _____   6. _____

C Work with your classmates. Make a list of the words from 2B.

PROBLEM SOLVING

A Listen. Look at the pictures.

Ivan's Problem

 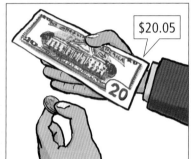

B Work with your classmates. Help Ivan.

a. Ask for a dime.   b. Go home.   c. Buy cheaper shoes.

UNIT **6**

FOCUS ON
• family members
• marital status
• the simple present
• talking about family and friends
• the U.S. school system

That's My Son

LESSON **1**   **Vocabulary**

1 Learn about friends and family members

A Look at the pictures. Count the men and women.

B Listen and point to the pictures.

C Listen and repeat the words.

1. parents	4. baby	7. friend
2. mother	5. girl	8. husband
3. father	6. boy	9. wife

D Read the new words with a partner.

2 Talk about families

A **Look at the picture. Complete the words.**

1. w _i_ f _e_

2. h ___ s ___ a n d

3. ___ a ___ h e r

4. p ___ r e n t ___

5. m ___ t h e ___

6. b a ___ y

7. b ___ y

8. ___ i r l

9. f r i ___ ___ d

B **Listen and repeat.**

1. **A:** Is this the father?
   B: No, that's the mother.

2. **A:** Is this the boy?
   B: Yes, that's the boy.

C **Work with a partner. Point to the people in 2A. Practice the conversations.**

A: Is this the _____?

B: No, that's the _____.

A: Is this the _____?

B: Yes, that's the _____.

TEST YOURSELF ✔

Close your book. Write 4 family words. Check your spelling in a dictionary.

1 Read about families

A **Look at the pictures. Point to the girls.**

Sandra

🎧 **B** **Listen and repeat the words.**

1. children
2. child
3. daughter
4. son
5. brother
6. sister

🎧 **C** **Listen and read Sandra's story.**

1. These are my children.
2. This is my son.
3. He's seven years old.
4. This is my daughter.
5. She's ten years old.

✔ Describe family members and marital status

D Listen to Freddy's story. Circle the correct word.

1. These are my ____.   (children)   child
2. This is my ____.   daughter   brother
3. ____ twenty years old.   He's   She's
4. This is my ____.   son   sister
5. ____ fifteen years old.   He's   She's

Freddy

2 Write about your family or friends

A Write about your family or friends. Complete the sentences. Show or draw a picture.

This is my _____.

He's _____ years old.

This is my _____.

She's _____ years old.

B Read your story to a partner.

3 Listen for marital status

A Listen and repeat the sentences.

We're married.   I'm single.   We're divorced.

B Listen. Circle *a* or *b*.

1. a. married   (b.) divorced   3. a. single   b. divorced
2. a. married   b. single   4. a. married   b. divorced

TEST YOURSELF ✔

Copy the sentences. Close your book. Then complete the sentences.
Use your own ideas.

This is my _____.   _____ is _____ years old.

1 Learn possessive adjectives

A Look at the pictures. Listen and read the sentences.

I am a student.
<u>My</u> name is Marie.

You are my friend.
<u>Your</u> name is Silvia.

He is my brother.
<u>His</u> name is Claude.

She is my sister.
<u>Her</u> name is Brigitte.

They are my friends.
<u>Their</u> names are Annie and Donna.

We are married.
<u>Our</u> names are Mr. and Mrs. Laurent.

B Complete the sentences. Circle *a* or *b*.

1. I'm a student. _____ name is Marie.

   a. Your   (b.) My

2. You are my friend. _____ name is Silvia.

   a. Your   b. My

3. He is my brother. _____ name is Claude.

   a. My   b. His

4. She is my sister. _____ name is Brigitte.

   a. His   b. Her

5. They are my friends. _____ names are Annie and Donna.

   a. Her   b. Their

6. We are married. _____ names are Mr. and Mrs. Laurent.

   a. Our   b. Their

C Read the sentences in 1B with a partner.

2 Learn the simple present

A Look at the pictures. Read the sentences.

He lives in California.

She lives in New York.

He lives in Texas.

They live in Florida.

B Study the chart. Listen and repeat.

I You	live	in New York.
He She	lives	
We They	live	

C Complete the sentences. Circle *a* or *b*.

1. I ____ in New York.
   (a.) live   b. lives

2. He ____ in New York.
   a. live   b. lives

3. They ____ in Minnesota.
   a. live   b. lives

4. You ____ in Washington.
   a. live   b. lives

D Complete the sentences. Use the simple present and possessive adjectives.

1. My brother ____lives____ in Texas. ____His____ name is Greg.

2. My sister _____ in Florida. _____ name is Barbara.

3. I _____ in New York. _____ name is Joe.

E Work with a partner. Talk about your family and friends.

My _____ lives in _____. _____ name is _____.

My _____ live in _____. Their names are _____.

TEST YOURSELF ✔

Write sentences about your family or friends. Compare your sentences with a partner.

My father lives in Mexico. His name is Antonio.

1 Learn to talk about families and friends

A Look at the pictures. Read the conversation.

B Listen and read.

Chang Sun:	Who's that?	**Nancy:**	Who's that?
Nancy:	That's my daughter.	**Chang Sun:**	That's my father.
Chang Sun:	What's her name?	**Nancy:**	What's his name?
Nancy:	Her name is Patricia.	**Chang Sun:**	His name is Lee.

C Listen again and repeat.

D Work with a partner. Practice the conversation. Use your own information. Show or draw a picture.

A: Who's that?

B: That's my _____.

A: What's _____ name?

B: _____ name is _____.

2 Listen for titles

 A Look at the pictures. Listen to the sentences.

1	2	3	4	5	6
I'm Mr. Jain. I'm single.	I'm Mr. Cohen. I'm married.	I'm Mrs. Cohen. I'm married.	I'm Miss Diaz. I'm single.	I'm Ms. Lim. I'm single.	I'm Ms. Flores. I'm married.

B Listen. Circle *a* or *b*.

1. (a.) I'm Mr. Jones.　　　b. I'm Mrs. Jones.

2. a. I'm Mr. Wong.　　　b. I'm Miss Wong.

3. a. I'm Mrs. Park.　　　b. I'm Ms. Park.

4. a. I'm Mrs. Chavez.　　b. I'm Mr. Chavez.

3 Real-life math

A Look at the ruler.

1 inch

| 1 | 2 | 3 | 4 | 5 | 6 | 7 | 8 | 9 | 10 | 11 | 12 |

12 inches = 1 foot

B Do the math and complete the sentence.

Her son is 10 years old. He is 50 inches tall.

Her son is ____ feet and ____ inches tall.

Need help?

1 foot
2 feet

TEST YOURSELF ✓

Copy the conversation. Close your book. Then add your own ideas and practice with a partner.

A: Who's that?
B: _____.

1 Learn about schools in the U.S.

A Look at the chart.

	Age	Grades	School
	5–6 years old	Kindergarten	Elementary school
	6–11 years old	First grade Third grade Second grade Fourth grade	Elementary school
		Fifth grade	Elementary or middle school
	11–14 years old	Sixth grade	Elementary or middle school
		Seventh grade Eighth grade	Middle or junior high school
	14–18 years old	Ninth grade Eleventh grade Tenth grade Twelfth grade	High school

B Complete the sentences. Circle *a* or *b*.

1. His daughter is eight years old. She's in ____ grade.
   a. eighth   (b.) third

2. Her son is five years old. He's in ____.
   a. fifth grade   b. kindergarten

3. Their son is in third grade. He's in ____.
   a. elementary school   b. high school

4. My daughter is in eleventh grade. She's ____ years old.
   a. eleven   b. seventeen

2 Get ready to read

A Look at the pictures. Read the words.

come

every day

on time

do homework

B Check (✔) the sentences about you.

☐ I come to class every day.

☐ I come to class on time.

☐ I do my homework.

3 Read a note

A Read the note from the teacher.

 Marshall Elementary School

Dear Mr. and Mrs. Santos,

Lila comes to class every day.
She comes to class on time.
She does her homework.
She is a good student.

Selma Romero

Ms. Selma Romero
Fourth-grade teacher

B Look at the note. Circle *a* or *b*.

1. Lila is in _____.

   a. third grade   (b.) fourth grade

2. Ms. Romero is the _____.

   a. mother   b. teacher

3. Mrs. Santos is the _____.

   a. mother   b. father

4. Lila is in _____.

   a. middle school   b. elementary school

BRING IT TO LIFE

Find the names of the elementary school, middle school (or junior high), and high school in your community. Tell the class.

First Elementary

King Middle School

Kent High School

1 Grammar

A Complete the sentences. Circle *a* or *b*.

1. He _____ to class on time.

   a. come   (b.) comes

2. She _____ in China.

   a. live   b. lives

3. I _____ in Illinois.

   a. live   b. lives

4. I _____ to class every day.

   a. come   b. comes

5. They _____ in North Carolina.

   a. live   b. lives

6. They _____ to class at 8:00.

   a. come   b. comes

B Complete the sentences. Use the words in the box.

Her   His   Their   Your   Our

1. He is my brother. _____His_____ name is Raja.

2. She is my sister. _____ name is Fatima.

3. You are my friend. _____ name is Alonso.

4. They are good students. _____ names are Oscar and Tina.

5. We are married. _____ names are Paul and Alicia.

2 Group work

A Work with 2–3 classmates. Look at the picture. Say what you see.

B Work with your group. Look at the picture in 2A again.
Write what you see. Check your spelling in a dictionary.

1. _____family_____   4. _____

2. _____   5. _____

3. _____   6. _____

C Work with your classmates. Make a list of the words from 2B.

PROBLEM SOLVING

A Listen. Look at the pictures.

Rosa's Problem

B Work with your classmates. Help Rosa.

a. Say, "No more baseball."

b. Say, "Only play baseball on Saturday."

c. Talk to the teacher.

Do we need apples?

FOCUS ON
- food
- food preferences
- the simple present
- asking for help in a store
- reading a shopping list

LESSON 1 **Vocabulary**

1 Learn about fruit and vegetables

A Look at the pictures. Say the prices.

B Listen and point to the pictures.

1	2	3
	$1.30	
4	5	6
$2.95		
7	8	9
		99¢

C Listen and repeat the words.

1. fruit
2. bananas
3. apples
4. grapes
5. oranges
6. vegetables
7. broccoli
8. cabbage
9. corn

D Read the new words with a partner.

2 Talk about fruit and vegetables

A Look at the picture. Complete the words.

1. b a n _a_ _n_ _a_ s
2. ____ r ____ p e s
3. o ____ a n g e ____
4. ____ p ____ l e s
5. ____ r u ____ t
6. ____ o ____ n
7. b r o c c ____ ____ i
8. c a b ____ ____ ____ e
9. ____ ____ g e ____ a b l e s

B Listen and repeat.

1. Where are the apples?
2. Where are the bananas?
3. Where are the grapes?
4. Where are the vegetables?

5. Where is the broccoli?
6. Where is the cabbage?
7. Where is the corn?
8. Where is the fruit?

C Work with a partner. Read the questions in 2B.
Point to the fruit and vegetables in 2A.

TEST YOURSELF ✔

Close your book. Write 2 words for fruit. Then write 2 words for vegetables.
Check your spelling in a dictionary.

1 Read about food

A Look at the pictures. What food do you see?

B Listen and repeat the words.

1. cheese	6. pork
2. eggs	7. beef
3. milk	8. lamb
4. bread	9. meat
5. chicken	10. rice

C Listen and read Barbara's story.

1. I like cheese.
2. I don't like pork.
3. My husband likes beef.
4. My daughter likes chicken.
5. We all like rice.

✔ Describe food preferences

D Listen to Don's story. Circle the correct word.

1. I like ____.   (meat)   milk
2. I don't like ____.   chicken   cheese
3. My wife likes ____.   lamb   rice
4. My son likes ____.   rice   eggs
5. We all like ____.   bread   beef

Don

2 Write about food you like

A Write about food. Complete the sentences. Use your own ideas.

I like _____.

I don't like _____.

My _____ likes _____.

My _____ likes _____.

B Read your story to a partner.

3 Listen for food groups

A Listen and check (✔) the boxes.

	fruit	vegetable	meat
pork			✔
grapes			
cabbage			

B Listen. Circle *a* or *b*.

1. a. pork   (b.) broccoli   4. a. cabbage   b. chicken
2. a. oranges   b. lamb   5. a. beef   b. bananas
3. a. grapes   b. corn   6. a. apples   b. corn

TEST YOURSELF ✓

Copy the sentences. Close your book. Then complete the sentences.
Use your own ideas.

I like _____. I don't like _____.

---

1 Learn negative statements with the simple present

A Look at the pictures. Read the sentences.

He likes rice and vegetables.
He doesn't like meat.

She likes bananas.
She doesn't like cabbage.

They like chicken.
They don't like rice.

B Study the chart. Listen and repeat.

I You	don't like	
He She	doesn't like	cabbage.
We They	don't like	

C Complete the sentences. Circle *a* or *b*. Then read the sentences with a partner.

1. I ____ cabbage.

   a. doesn't like   (b.) don't like

2. She ____ cabbage.

   a. doesn't like   b. don't like

3. They ____ bananas.

   a. doesn't like   b. don't like

4. He ____ pork.

   a. doesn't like   b. don't like

5. I ____ lamb.

   a. doesn't like   b. don't like

6. We ____ broccoli.

   a. doesn't like   b. don't like

D Complete the sentences. Use *don't* or *doesn't*.

1. I ___*don't*___ like bananas.

2. She _____ like cheese.

3. He _____ like fruit.

4. They _____ like pork.

✔ Use the simple present to express likes, dislikes, and needs

2 Learn *Yes/No* questions with the simple present

A Listen and look at the pictures. Read the conversations.

A: <u>Do you need</u> rice?
B: Yes, <u>I do</u>.
A: <u>Do you need</u> bread?
B: No, <u>I don't</u>.

A: <u>Does he need</u> milk?
B: Yes, <u>he does</u>.
A: <u>Does he need</u> eggs?
B: No, <u>he doesn't</u>.

A: <u>Do they need</u> oranges?
B: Yes, <u>they do</u>.
A: <u>Do they need</u> apples?
B: No, <u>they don't</u>.

A: <u>Do we need</u> broccoli?
B: Yes, <u>we do</u>.
A: <u>Do we need</u> cabbage?
B: No, <u>we don't</u>.

B Match the questions with the answers.

_c_ 1. Do you need rice?   a. No, they don't.

___ 2. Does she need chicken?   b. Yes, he does.

___ 3. Do they need apples?   c. Yes, I do.

___ 4. Does he need broccoli?   d. No, she doesn't.

C Complete the questions. Use *Do* or *Does*.

1. ___Does___ she need rice?   4. _____ she like pork?

2. _____ they need grapes?   5. _____ they like chicken?

3. _____ you like cabbage?   6. _____ we need eggs?

D Work with a partner. Ask and answer the questions in 2C.
Use your own ideas.

TEST YOURSELF ✔

Write questions with *like*. Write the answers. Compare your questions and answers with a partner.

Do you like bananas? Yes, I do.

1 Learn to ask for help in a store

A Look at the pictures. Read the conversation.

Can I help you?
Yes, I need apples.
Clerk
Rosita

Here you go.

Thanks.
You're welcome.

B Listen and read.

Clerk: Can I help you?
Rosita: Yes, I need apples.
Clerk: Here you go.
Rosita: Thanks.
Clerk: You're welcome.

C Listen again and repeat.

D Work with a partner. Practice the conversation. Use your own ideas.

A: Can I help you?

B: Yes, I need _____.

A: Here you go.

B: Thanks.

A: You're welcome.

Need help?

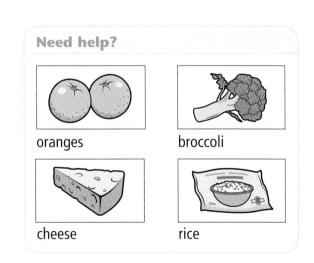
oranges   broccoli

cheese   rice

2 Listen for prices

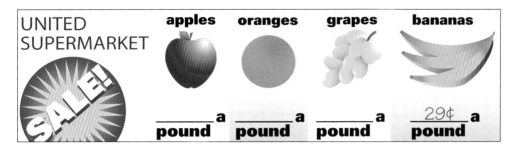

🎧 **A** Listen and point to the food.

UNITED SUPERMARKET

SALE!

apples _____ a pound

oranges _____ a pound

grapes _____ a pound

bananas ___29¢___ a pound

🎧 **B** Listen again. Write the prices in the ad in 2A.

C Work with a partner. Ask about the prices.

A: *Are the bananas expensive?*
B: *No, they're not. They're cheap.*

3 Real-life math

A Look at the ad. Read the prices.

Apples   3 lbs. for $2   **Oranges   5 lbs. for $3**

> **Need help?**
>
> lb. = pound
> lbs. = pounds

B Read the problems. Do the math. Write the prices.

1. Jane needs 6 pounds of apples.

   3 lbs. x 2 = 6 lbs.

   $2 x 2 = $__4__

   6 lbs. of apples = $____

2. Azim needs 10 pounds of oranges.

   5 lbs. x ____ = 10 lbs.

   $3 x 2 = $____

   10 lbs. of oranges = $____

TEST YOURSELF ✔

Copy the conversation. Close your book. Then add your own ideas and practice with a partner.

A: *Excuse me. I need _____.*
B: _____.

1 Learn about containers

A Look at the pictures. Listen and repeat.

a can of coffee

a can of soup

a bottle of water

a bottle of juice

a box of cereal

a box of tea

B Listen. Circle *a* or *b*.

1. a. can   b. box   4. a. can   b. bottle
2. a. bottle   b. box   5. a. box   b. bottle
3. a. can   b. bottle   6. a. box   b. can

2 Get ready to read

A Look at the pictures. Read the words.

buy

shopping

B Check (✔) the sentence about you.

☐ I like shopping.

☐ I don't like shopping.

3 Read a shopping list

A Read the shopping list.

Need help?

box

boxes

B Look at the shopping list. Circle *a* or *b*.

1. Do they need soup?

   a. No, they don't.   (b.) Yes, they do.

2. Do they need cabbage?

   a. No, they don't.   b. Yes, they do.

3. Do they need orange juice?

   a. No, they don't.   b. Yes, they do.

4. Do they need fruit?

   a. No, they don't.   b. Yes, they do.

5. Do they need milk?

   a. No, they don't.   b. Yes, they do.

BRING IT TO LIFE

Bring a shopping list to class. Talk about the food you need.

Shopping List
coffee (1 can)
water (6 bottles)
juice (2 bottles)
tea
cereal (3 boxes)
apples
corn

1 Grammar

A Complete the sentences. Use *don't like* or *doesn't like*.

1. He _____doesn't like_____ lamb.

2. They _____ cheese.

3. She _____ oranges.

4. I _____ corn.

B Complete the questions and answers. Use *do, don't, does,* or *doesn't*.

1. A: ___Does___ he need broccoli?

   B: Yes, he does.

2. A: _____ she need pork?

   B: No, she doesn't.

3. A: _____ they need juice?

   B: Yes, they do.

4. A: _____ they need coffee?

   B: No, they don't.

5. A: Does he like vegetables?

   B: Yes, he _____.

6. A: Do you like lamb?

   B: No, I _____.

7. A: Does she like eggs?

   B: No, she _____.

8. A: Do they need cheese?

   B: Yes, they _____.

2 Group work

A Work with 2–3 classmates. Look at the picture. Say what you see.

B Work with your group. Look at the picture in 2A again. Write what you see. Check your spelling in a dictionary.

1. _____broccoli_____   4. _____

2. _____   5. _____

3. _____   6. _____

C Work with your classmates. Make a list of the words from 2B.

PROBLEM SOLVING

A Listen. Look at the pictures.

Duncan's Problem

6 a.m.   12 p.m.   8 p.m.   10 p.m.

B Work with your classmates. Help Duncan.

a. Eat breakfast at home.   b. Make lunch.   c. Walk to work.

UNIT 8

Take Two Tablets

FOCUS ON
- parts of the body
- symptoms and ailments
- *have* and *has*
- making a doctor's appointment
- reading medicine labels

LESSON 1 Vocabulary

1 Learn parts of the body

A Look at the picture. Is she sick?

B Listen and point to the picture.

C Listen and repeat the words.

1. head	4. nose	7. hand
2. eye	5. arm	8. leg
3. ear	6. stomach	9. foot

D Read the new words with a partner.

2 Talk about parts of the body

A Look at the picture. Complete the words.

1. h e _a_ _d_

2. e a ____

3. e y ____

4. ____ ____ s e

5. h ____ n ____

6. a r ____

7. s ____ ____ m a c h

8. ____ o o ____

9. ____ e g

B Look at the pictures. Listen and follow the directions.

Point to your head.

Point to your leg.

C Work with a partner. Give directions. Listen and follow your partner's directions.

Point to your _____.

TEST YOURSELF ✔

Close your book. Write 4 parts of the body. Check your spelling in a dictionary.

1 Read about health problems

A Look at the picture. What parts of the body do you see?

B Listen and repeat the words.

1. a cold
2. a cough
3. an earache
4. a sore throat
5. a headache
6. a stomachache
7. a fever
8. the flu

C Listen and read Paula's story.

1. My family is sick.
2. My daughter has a cold.
3. My son has an earache.
4. My husband has a sore throat.
5. I have a headache.

D Listen to Carl's story. Circle the correct word.

1. My family is ____.   sad   (sick)
2. My brother has ____.   a fever   the flu
3. My sister has ____.   a sore throat a stomachache
4. My mother has ____.   a cold   a cough
5. I have ____.   a cold   a cough

Carl

2 Write about health problems

A Write about health problems. Complete the sentences.
Use your own ideas.

My _____ has _____.

My _____ has _____.

My _____ has _____.

I have _____.

B Read your story to a partner.

3 Listen and complete a medical form

A Listen and point to the health problems you hear.

Daniela Lopez
name
☑ cough   ☐ earache
☐ fever   ☐ sore throat
☐ headache   ☐ flu
☐ other: _____

Charlie Foss
name
☐ cough   ☐ earache
☐ fever   ☐ sore throat
☐ headache   ☐ flu
☐ other: _____

B Listen again. Check (✔) the health problems you hear.

TEST YOURSELF ✔

Copy the sentences. Close your book. Then complete the sentences.
Use your own ideas.

I have _____.   He has _____.

1 Learn *have* and *has*

A Look at the pictures. Read the sentences.

He has a sore throat.

She has a fever.

She has an earache.

B Study the chart. Listen and repeat.

I You	have	the flu.
He She	has	
We They	have	

C Complete the sentences. Use *have* or *has*. Then read the sentences with a partner.

1. I _____have_____ the flu.

2. He _____ the flu.

3. She _____ the flu.

4. They _____ the flu.

5. Matt _____ a headache.

6. Jill _____ a stomachache.

D Look at the pictures. Complete the sentences. Use *has* or *have* and the health problem.

1. She _____.

2. He _____.

✔ Use *have* and *has* to describe symptoms and ailments

2 Learn *Yes/No* questions with *have*

A Look at the pictures. Listen to the questions and answers.

Dr. Tam: <u>Do you have</u> a sore throat?
Eva: <u>Yes, I do.</u>
Dr. Tam: <u>Do you have</u> a stomachache?
Eva: <u>No, I don't.</u>

Dr. Garcia: <u>Does he have</u> a fever?
Flor: <u>Yes, he does.</u>
Dr. Garcia: <u>Does he have</u> an earache?
Flor: <u>No, he doesn't.</u>

Dr. Barr: <u>Do they have</u> coughs?
Vinh: <u>Yes, they do.</u>
Dr. Barr: <u>Do they have</u> fevers?
Vinh: <u>No, they don't.</u>

Girls: <u>Do we have</u> fevers?
Dr. Cantu: <u>No, you don't.</u>
Girls: <u>Do we have</u> the flu?
Dr. Cantu: <u>No, you don't.</u>

B Complete the questions and answers.

1. A: ____<u>Does he have</u>____ a sore throat?

   B: Yes, he does.

2. A: _____ a stomachache?

   B: No, I don't.

3. A: Does he have the flu?

   B: Yes, _____.

4. A: Does he have an earache?

   B: No, _____.

C Complete the questions and sentences. Use *have* or *has*.

1. Does he ____<u>have</u>____ a cough?

2. Do you _____ the flu?

3. She _____ a cold.

4. I _____ a headache.

5. He _____ a stomachache.

6. Does she _____ a sore throat?

D Work with a partner. Read the conversations in 2B.

TEST YOURSELF ✔

Write questions and answers about health problems. Compare your
questions and answers with a partner.

Does Olivia have a headache? No, she doesn't.

1 Learn how to make a doctor's appointment

A Look at the pictures. Read the conversation.

B Listen and read.

Receptionist: Hello, Downtown Clinic.
Kara: This is Kara Woods. I need to see the doctor.
Receptionist: What's the matter?
Kara: I have a stomachache.
Receptionist: Is 2:00 OK?
Kara: Yes, thank you.

C Listen again and repeat.

D Work with a partner. Practice the conversation. Use your own ideas.

A: Hello, Downtown Clinic.

B: Hello. I need to see the doctor.

A: What's the matter?

B: I have a _____.

A: Is _____ OK?

B: Yes, thank you.

Need help?

fever   headache

cough   earache

2 Listen for medical appointment information

A Listen to the phone calls. Point to the days you hear.

Doctor's Appointment Book

	Monday	Tuesday	Wednesday	Thursday	Friday
8:00			✔		
8:30					
9:00					
9:30					

B Listen again. Check (✔) the day and time in the calendar.

3 Practice your pronunciation

A Listen for the different sounds of *a*.

m<u>a</u>tter	<u>a</u>che
have	say
has	name
sad	plane
hand	

B Listen and write these words in the chart.

~~hand~~	grapes	happy	day

C Listen again and check your answers.

TEST YOURSELF ✔

Copy the conversation. Close your book. Then add your own
ideas and practice with a partner.

A: Hello. This is _____.
B: _____.

---

1 Learn about frequency

A Look at the calendars. Listen and repeat.

every day

twice a day

three times a day

every six hours

every four hours

B Match the frequency with the times.

<u> c </u> 1. every four hours   a. 8 a.m., 8 p.m.

_____ 2. every day   b. 8 a.m., 2 p.m., 8 p.m., 2 a.m.

_____ 3. every six hours   c. 8 a.m., 12 p.m., 4 p.m., 8 p.m., 12 a.m., 4 a.m.

_____ 4. twice a day   d. 8 a.m., 4 p.m., 12 a.m.

_____ 5. three times a day   e. Sun., Mon., Tues., Wed., Thurs., Fri., Sat.

2 Get ready to read

A Look at the pictures. Read the words.

medicine

label

teaspoon

tablespoon

tablet

B What medicine do you have at home? Check (✔) the boxes.

☐ I have medicine for headaches.

☐ I have medicine for earaches.

☐ I have medicine for coughs.

3 Read medicine labels

A Read the medicine labels.

Take 2 tablespoons every 6 hours.

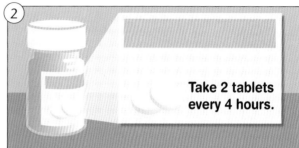

Take 2 tablets every 4 hours.

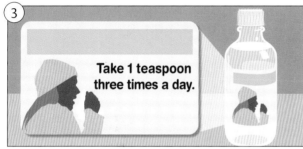

Take 1 teaspoon three times a day.

Take 1 tablespoon twice a day.

B Look at the medicine labels. Circle *a* or *b*.

1. Medicine 1: ____.

   a. take six tablespoons   (b.) take two tablespoons

2. Medicine 2: ____.

   a. take every two hours   b. take every four hours

3. Medicine 3: ____.

   a. take three times a day   b. take every three hours

4. Medicine 4: ____.

   a. take one teaspoon   b. take one tablespoon

BRING IT TO LIFE

Bring in medicine from the store or from a doctor.
Circle one new word.

1 Grammar

A **Complete the sentences. Use *have* or *has*.**

1. He _____has_____ a headache.

2. She _____ a sore throat.

3. They _____ the flu.

4. I _____ a stomachache.

5. He _____ a cold.

6. We _____ fevers.

B **Complete the questions and answers.**

1. **A:** Do you have a fever?

   B: Yes, _____I do_____.

2. **A:** Does she have a cold?

   B: Yes, _____.

3. **A:** Do they have the flu?

   B: Yes, _____.

4. **A:** _____ a cough?

   B: Yes, I do.

5. **A:** _____ a sore throat?

   B: Yes, he does.

6. **A:** _____ a headache?

   B: Yes, she does.

2 Group work

A **Work with 2–3 classmates. Look at the picture. Say what you see.**

B Work with your group. Look at the picture in 2A again.
Write what you see. Check your spelling in a dictionary.

1. _____*headache*_____   4. _____

2. _____   5. _____

3. _____   6. _____

C Work with your classmates. Make a list of the words from 2B.

PROBLEM SOLVING

A Listen. Look at the pictures.

Orane's Problem

B Work with your classmates. Help Orane.

a. Go to work.   b. Go to the doctor.   c. Stay home.

What size?

FOCUS ON
- colors
- clothes
- the present continuous
- shopping for clothes
- weather

LESSON **1** Vocabulary

1 Learn colors

A Look at the pictures. Count the shoes.

🎧 **B** Listen and point to the colors.

🎧 **C** Listen and repeat the words.

1. black	4. blue	7. brown
2. white	5. yellow	8. orange
3. red	6. green	9. purple

D Read the new words with a partner.

2 Talk about colors

A **Look at the picture. Complete the words.**

1. r _e_ d

2. g r ___ e ___

3. ___ h i ___ e

4. b ___ ___ c k

5. ___ r ___ w ___

6. ___ r ___ n g ___

7. y ___ l ___ o w

8. ___ l ___ e

9. ___ u ___ p l e

B **Listen and repeat.**

A: What color is this sweater?
B: It's red.
A: What color is this shirt?
B: It's purple.

C **Work with a partner. Point to the clothes in 2A. Practice the conversation.**

A: What color is this _____?

B: It's _____.

TEST YOURSELF ✔

Close your book. Write 5 colors. Check your spelling in a dictionary.

1 Read about clothes

A Look at the pictures. Say the months.

July

October

February

B Listen and repeat the words.

1. cap
2. T-shirt
3. shorts
4. jacket
5. dress
6. coat
7. belt
8. boots

C Listen and read Justine's story.

1. It's July.
2. I'm wearing white shorts.
3. I'm wearing a red T-shirt.
4. I'm wearing a blue cap.

D Listen to Ben's story. Circle the correct word.

1. It's ____.   (January)   June

2. I'm wearing a blue ____.   cap   coat

3. I'm wearing brown ____.   boots   belt

4. I'm wearing a brown ____.   belt   boot   Ben

2 Write about your clothes

A Write about your clothes. Complete the sentences. Use your own ideas.

I'm wearing _____.

I'm wearing _____.

I'm wearing _____.

B Read your story to a partner.

3 Listen for clothes and colors

A Listen. Circle *a* or *b*.

1. a.   b.   3. a.   b.

2. a.   b.   4. a.   b.

B Work with a partner. Talk about the pictures in 1A and 3A.

It's a red dress. It's a red sweater.

TEST YOURSELF ✔

Copy the sentences. Close your book. Then complete the sentences. Use your own ideas.

It's March. I'm wearing _____. It's June. I'm wearing _____.

1 Learn statements with the present continuous

A Look at the pictures. Read the sentences.

I am wearing black pants.

She is wearing a blue dress.

It is wearing shoes.

B Study the chart. Listen and repeat.

I	am		
You	are		
He She It	is	wearing	shoes.
We They	are		

C Complete the sentences. Circle *a* or *b*.

1. I ____ wearing shoes.
   a. is   (b.) am

2. You ____ wearing shoes.
   a. are   b. is

3. He ____ wearing black pants.
   a. are   b. is

4. They ____ wearing red caps.
   a. are   b. is

D Complete the sentences. Use *is wearing* or *are wearing*.
Then read the sentences with a partner.

1. She _____*is wearing*_____ a green sweater.

2. They _____ white coats.

3. He _____ blue pants.

4. You _____ a purple dress.

2 Learn *Yes/No* questions with the present continuous

A Look at the pictures. Listen and read the questions and answers.

A: <u>Are you wearing a dress?</u>
B: Yes, I am.

A: <u>Is Ed reading a book?</u>
B: Yes, he is.

A: <u>Is Min reading a book?</u>
B: No, she's not.

A: <u>Is the cat sleeping?</u>
B: Yes, it is.

A: <u>Are we going to the library?</u>
B: No, we're not.

A: <u>Are they wearing red shoes?</u>
B: No, they're not.

B Complete the questions. Use the present continuous.

1. A: _____Are_____ you wearing a skirt?

   B: Yes, I am.

2. A: _____ Irene wearing an orange T-shirt?

   B: Yes, she is.

3. A: Is Cho _____ brown shoes?

   B: Yes, he is.

4. A: Is Ana _____ a jacket?

   B: Yes, she is.

C Work with a partner. Read the conversations in 2A and 2B.

TEST YOURSELF ✔

Write questions and answers about your classmates. Compare your sentences
with a partner.

Is Galina wearing a dress? No, she's not.
Is Azim wearing blue pants? Yes, he is.

1 Learn about shopping for clothes

A Look at the pictures. Read the conversation.

B Listen and read.

Hector: Excuse me. I'm looking for a T-shirt.
Clerk: What size?
Hector: Small.
Clerk: Here's a small.
Hector: Thanks.

C Listen again and repeat.

D Work with a partner. Practice the conversation. Use your own ideas.

A: I'm looking for a _____.

B: What size?

A: _____.

B: Here's a _____.

A: Thanks.

Need help?

small   medium

large   extra-large

2 Listen for sizes

A Look at the picture. What color are the T-shirts?

B Listen. Circle *a* or *b*.

1. a. large   (b.) extra-large   3. a. large   b. medium
2. a. small   b. medium   4. a. small   b. extra-large

C Listen. Find the picture. Write the prices.

_$12.99_

3 Real-life math

A Read the receipt. Answer the questions.

1. How much is the dress? _____

2. How much is the jacket? _____

3. How much is the tax? _____

B Do the math. Write the total on the receipt.

The Clothes Spot

dress	$35.00
jacket	$30.00
sub-total	$65.00
tax 5%	$3.25
Total	_____

TEST YOURSELF ✔

Copy the conversation. Close your book. Then add your own ideas and practice with a partner.

A: I'm looking for a _____.
B: What _____?

1 Learn about the weather

🎧 **A** **Look at the pictures. Listen and repeat.**

It's sunny.   It's cloudy.   It's raining.   It's snowing.

B **Look at the pictures. Complete the sentences.**

1. It's _____sunny_____. He's wearing shorts.

2. It's _____. She's reading a book.

3. It's _____. They're playing soccer.

4. It's _____. He's sleeping.

2 Get ready to read

A **Look at the pictures. Read the sentences.**

It's hot.   It's warm.   It's cool.   It's cold.

B Check (✔) your favorite weather.

☐ hot ☐ cool

☐ warm ☐ cold

3 Read a weather website

A Read the website.

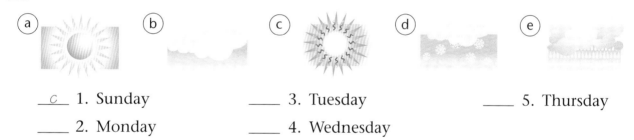

The Weather This Week				
Address: @ http://www.weatherthisweek.us				
Sunday	**Monday**	**Tuesday**	**Wednesday**	**Thursday**
Sunny and hot	Sunny and warm	Cloudy and cool	Raining and cool	Snowing and cold

B Match the weather with the days.

ⓐ   ⓑ   ⓒ   ⓓ   ⓔ

_c_ 1. Sunday ___ 3. Tuesday ___ 5. Thursday

___ 2. Monday ___ 4. Wednesday

C Write or draw about the weather for your city this week.

Sunday	Monday	Tuesday	Wednesday	Thursday

BRING IT TO LIFE

Bring a weather page from the newspaper or the Internet to class. Circle one new word.

1 Grammar

A **Match the questions with the answers.**

_c_ 1. Are you looking for a T-shirt?

____ 2. Is it raining?

____ 3. Is she sleeping?

____ 4. Is he wearing a coat?

____ 5. Are they wearing boots?

a. Yes, she is.

b. No, he's not.

c. Yes, I am.

d. No, they're not.

e. Yes, it is.

B **Complete the questions and sentences. Circle *a* or *b*.**

1. ____ looking for a T-shirt?

   a. Are you   b. You are

2. ____ wearing jackets?

   a. They are   b. Are they

3. ____ snowing?

   a. Is it   b. It is

4. ____ wearing a coat.

   a. He is   b. Is he

5. ____ raining.

   a. Is it   b. It is

6. ____ wearing a brown belt.

   a. You are   b. Are you

2 Group work

A **Work with 2–3 classmates. Look at the pictures. Say what you see.**

B Work with your group. Look at the pictures in 2A again. Write what you see. Check your spelling in a dictionary.

1. _____boots_____
2. _____
3. _____

4. _____
5. _____
6. _____

C Work with your classmates. Make a list of the words from 2B.

PROBLEM SOLVING

A Listen. Look at the pictures.

Ethan's Problem

B Work with your classmates. Help Ethan.

a. Wear it.

b. Put it in the closet.

c. Return it.

d. Other: _____

UNIT 10

Where's the bank?

FOCUS ON
- places in the community
- locations
- *There is* and *There are*
- asking for and giving locations
- community services

LESSON 1 Vocabulary

1 Learn places in the community

A Look at the pictures. Say what you see.

🎧 **B** Listen and point to the pictures.

🎧 **C** Listen and repeat the words.

1. bookstore
2. bus station
3. drugstore
4. laundromat
5. park
6. bank
7. post office
8. restaurant
9. supermarket

D Read the new words with a partner.

2 Talk about places in the community

A Look at the picture. Complete the words.

1. _p_ o s t   o _f_ _f_ i c e

2. b ___ n ___

3. s u ___ e r m a ___ k e t

4. p ___ r ___

5. l ___ ___ n d ___ o m a t

6. b ___ o k s ___ o ___ e

7. r e s ___ ___ u r a n ___

8. ___ r ___ g s t o ___ e

9. b u s   s ___ a t ___ ___ n

B Listen and repeat.

1. **A:** Is this the bus station?
   B: No, it's the post office.

2. **A:** Is this the drugstore?
   B: Yes, it is.

C Work with a partner. Point to the places in 2A.
Practice the conversations.

1. **A:** Is this the _____?
   B: No, it's the _____.

2. **A:** Is this the _____?
   B: Yes, it is.

TEST YOURSELF ✔

Close your book. Write 4 places in the community.
Check your spelling in a dictionary.

1 Read about locations in the community

A Look at the picture. Point to the park.

B Listen and repeat the words.

1. apartment building
2. house
3. between
4. across from
5. next to
6. on the corner

C Listen and read Pat's story.

1. My apartment building is on Pine Street.
2. There is a laundromat across from the apartment building.
3. There is a restaurant next to the laundromat.
4. There is a park on the corner.
5. I go to the park on Saturdays.

D Listen to Rob's story. Circle the correct word.

1. My house is ____ Third Street.   (on)   in

2. There is a park ____ the house.   across from   next to

3. There is a post office ____ the park.   across from   next to

4. There is a bank ____ the corner.   on   in

5. I go to the ____ on Sundays.   bookstore   drugstore   Rob

2 Write about a street

A Write about a street you know. Complete the sentences.

There is a _____ across from the _____.

There is a _____ next to the _____.

There is a _____ on the corner.

B Read your story to a partner.

3 Listen for locations

A Listen and complete the sentences. Use the words in the box.

across from   ~~next to~~   corner   between

1. The park is _____ _next to_ _____ the house.

2. The laundromat is _____ the apartment building.

3. The house is _____ the park and the apartment building.

4. The park is on the _____.

B Work with a partner. Talk about the picture in 1A.

The park is across from the houses.

> **TEST YOURSELF** ✔
> Copy the sentences. Close your book. Then complete the sentences.
> Use your own ideas.

1 Learn statements with *There is* and *There are*

A Look at the pictures. Read the sentences.

There is a supermarket next
to the restaurant.

There are two schools on
Ash Street.

B Study the chart. Listen and repeat.

There is	a supermarket	on Green Street.
	a post office	
There are	two banks	
	three restaurants	

C Complete the sentences. Use *is* or *are*.

1. There _____is_____ a supermarket on Green Street.

2. There _____ a post office on Green Street.

3. There _____ two banks on Green Street.

4. There _____ three restaurants on Green Street.

D Complete the sentences. Use *There is* or *There are*.

1. _____There is_____ a bank next to the restaurant.

2. _____ two restaurants between the bank and the bookstore.

3. _____ a restaurant on the corner.

4. _____ a drugstore across from the restaurant.

5. _____ two banks on Walnut Street.

2 Learn *Yes/No* questions with *Is there*

A Listen and look at the pictures. Read the conversations.

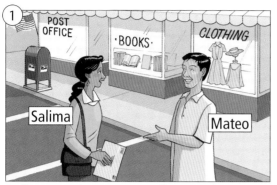

Salima: Is there a post office nearby?
Mateo: Yes, there is.

Jia: Is there a supermarket nearby?
Dolores: No, there isn't.

B Look at the pictures in 2A. Circle *a* or *b*.

1. Is there a post office nearby?
   a. Yes, there is.   b. Yes, it is.

2. Is there a supermarket nearby?
   a. No, it isn't.   b. No, there isn't.

3. Is there a bookstore nearby?
   a. Yes, there is.   b. No, there isn't.

4. Is there a drugstore nearby?
   a. Yes, there is.   b. No, there isn't.

C Complete the questions.

1. _____Is there_____ a park nearby?

2. _____ a laundromat nearby?

3. _____ a bus station nearby?

4. _____ a library nearby?

D Work with a partner. Talk about your community.

1. **A:** Is there a _____ nearby?

   B: Yes, there is.

2. **A:** Is there a _____ nearby?

   B: No, there isn't.

TEST YOURSELF ✔

Write questions and answers about your community.
Compare your sentences with a partner.

Is there a bus station nearby? Yes, there is.

1 Learn to talk about locations

A **Look at the pictures. Read the conversation.**

B **Listen and read.**

Mario: Excuse me. Where is the drugstore?

Phu: It's next to the bookstore.

Mario: Thank you.

Phu: You're welcome.

C **Listen again and repeat.**

D **Work with a partner. Practice the conversation. Use your own ideas.**

A: Excuse me. Where is the _____?

B: It's _____.

A: Thank you.

B: You're welcome.

2 Listen for locations

A Look at the map. Listen and point to the places.

B Listen again. Write the places on the map. Use the words in the box.

~~drugstore~~   bookstore   restaurant   park

3 Real-life math

A Look at the map. Read the sentences.

1. Freemont is 9 miles from Tipton.
2. Tipton is 12 miles from Greenville.

B Look at the map in 3A. Do the math. Complete the sentence.

9 + 12 = ____   Freemont is ____ miles from Greenville.

TEST YOURSELF ✔

Copy the conversation. Close your book. Then add your
own ideas and practice with a partner.

A: Excuse me. Where is the _____?
B: _____.

1 Learn about community services

A Look at the pictures. Listen and repeat.

Department of Motor Vehicles (DMV)

police station

fire station

hospital

ambulance

courthouse

B Listen. Circle *a* or *b*.

1. a. b.
2. a. b.

3. a. b.
4. a. b.

2 Get ready to read

A Look at the pictures. Read the words.

emergency

non-emergency

town@ca.gov
email address

directory

B Work with your classmates. Look at the pictures.
Circle *emergency* or *non-emergency*.

emergency   non-emergency

emergency   non-emergency

3 Read a city-services directory

A Read the city-services directory.

Lakewood City Directory

Police

Fire

Ambulance and Hospital

EMERGENCY NUMBER
911

Non-emergency numbers

Hospital	311 First Street	(505) 555-9111	
Police Station	1324 Adams Street	(505) 555-1010	
Fire Station	831 Third Street	(505) 555-0985	
DMV	389 Second Street	(505) 555-3421	email address: dmv@lakewood.us
Courthouse	3251 Third Street	(505) 555-1900	email address: court@lakewood.us

B Look at the directory. Circle *a* or *b*.

1. For a police emergency, call ____.
   a. 911   b. (505) 555-1010
2. The hospital is on ____.
   a. Adams Street   b. First Street
3. The fire station is on ____.
   a. First Street   b. Third Street
4. The non-emergency number for the hospital is ____.
   a. (505) 555-9111   b. 911

BRING IT TO LIFE

Find the phone number for your police station. Bring it to class.

Midtown Police
(677) 555-9889

1 Grammar

A Complete the sentences. Use *There is* or *There are*.

1. _____There is_____ a park on Second Street.

2. _____ two banks nearby.

3. _____ a post office on the corner.

4. _____ two restaurants next to the hospital.

5. _____ a library next to the DMV.

B Complete the questions and answers.

1. **A:** _____Is there_____ a police station nearby?

   B: Yes, there is.

2. **A:** _____ a fire station on the corner?

   B: No, there isn't.

3. **A:** _____ a park next to the school?

   B: Yes, _____.

4. **A:** _____ a restaurant nearby?

   B: No, _____.

2 Group work

A Work with 2–3 classmates. Look at the picture. Say what you see.

B Work with your group. Look at the picture in 2A again. Write what you see. Check your spelling in a dictionary.

1. _____restaurant_____ 4. _____

2. _____ 5. _____

3. _____ 6. _____

C Work with your classmates. Make a list of the words from 2B.

PROBLEM SOLVING

A Listen. Look at the picture.

Elena's Problem

B Work with your classmates. Help Elena.

a. Call the police.

b. Go out.

c. Listen to music.

d. Other: _____

UNIT **11**

This Is My Home

FOCUS ON
- things in the home
- rooms in a home
- possessive 's
- asking about a home for rent
- reading a classified ad

LESSON 1 Vocabulary

1 Learn words for things in the home

A Look at the pictures. What food do you see?

B Listen and point to the pictures.

①	②	③
④	⑤	⑥
⑦	⑧	⑨

C Listen and repeat the words.

1. room
2. window
3. furniture
4. sofa
5. bed
6. dresser
7. TV
8. stove
9. refrigerator

D Read the new words with a partner.

2 Talk about your home

A Look at the pictures. Complete the words.

1. __r__ o o __m__

2. r e f ___ ___ g e r a ___ ___ r

3. ___ t o ___ e

4. d r ___ s ___ e r

5. ___ e d

6. f u r ___ i ___ ___ r e

7. w ___ n ___ ___ w

8. T ___

9. s ___ ___ a

B Listen and repeat.

1. **A:** Where's the stove?
   B: It's next to the refrigerator.

2. **A:** Where's the TV?
   B: It's across from the sofa.

C Work with a partner. Point to the pictures in 2A. Practice the conversation.

A: Where's the _____?

B: It's _____.

TEST YOURSELF ✔

Close your book. Write 3 furniture words and 3 things in the home.
Check your spelling in a dictionary.

1 Read about a home

A Look at the picture. What furniture do you see?

B Listen and repeat the words.

1. on
2. in
3. bedroom
4. bathroom
5. living room
6. above
7. below
8. kitchen
9. garage

C Listen and read Peter's story.

1. This is my home.
2. There is one bedroom and one bathroom.
3. There is a blue sofa in the living room.
4. There are two windows above the sofa.
5. I like my home.

🎧 **D** **Listen to Meg's story. Circle the correct word.**

1. ____ is my home.   (This)   There

2. There are three ____.   bathrooms   bedrooms

3. There is a table in the ____.   kitchen   garage

4. There is a window ____ the table.   below   above

5. I like my ____.   living room   bedroom

Meg

2 Write about your home

A **Write about your home. Complete the sentences. Draw a picture.**

This is my home.

There _____.

There is a _____ in the _____.

There is a _____ above the _____.

B **Read your story to a partner.**

3 Listen for locations in the home

🎧 **A** **Listen and draw the furniture in the room.**

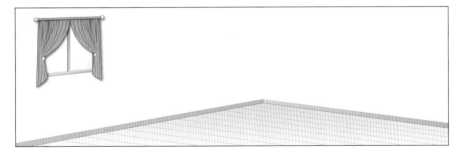

B **Work with a partner. Talk about the picture in 3A.**

The bed is next to the dresser.

┌─ **TEST YOURSELF** ✔ ─────────────────────────────────────

Copy the sentences. Close your book. Then complete the sentences.
Use your own ideas.

There is a _____ in the _____.
There is a _____ above the _____.

1 Learn possessive 's

A Look at the pictures. Listen and read the sentences.

Teng's house is white.

Gloria's home is small.

Mr. and Mrs. Smith's home is big.

Karen's bedroom is green.

B Match the sentences.

_c_ 1. His house is white.

_____ 2. Her home is small.

_____ 3. Their home is big.

_____ 4. Her bedroom is green.

_____ 5. His living room is big.

a. Lionel's living room is big.

b. Karen's bedroom is green.

c. Teng's house is white.

d. Mr. and Mrs. Smith's home is big.

e. Gloria's home is small.

C Look at the pictures. Complete the sentences.
Write about the pictures.

Min

Alba

Taylor

Mr. and Mrs. Brown

1. _____Min's_____ kitchen is small.

2. _____ sofa is purple.

3. _____ living room is black and white.

4. _____ TV is in the kitchen.

2 Learn questions with *How many*

A **Read the conversation.**

A: How many chairs are there in the living room?

B: One.

B **Study the chart. Listen and repeat.**

How many	chairs	are there	in the living room?
	windows		

C **Complete the questions. Circle *a* or *b*. Then read the questions with a partner.**

1. How many ____ are there in the living room?

   a. chair   (b.) chairs

2. How many ____ are there in the living room?

   a. windows   b. window

3. How many ____ are there?

   a. bedroom   b. bedrooms

4. How many ____ are there?

   a. beds   b. bed

5. How many ____ are there in Sally's home?

   a. bathroom   b. bathrooms

6. How many ____ are there in Flora's house?

   a. TVs   b. TV

D **Work with a partner. Look at the pictures in 1A and 1C. Ask and answer questions.**

How many _____ are there _____?

TEST YOURSELF ✔

Write questions and answers about the pictures in 1A or 1C.
Compare your sentences with your partner.

How many sofas are there in Alba's home? One.

1 Learn to ask about a home for rent

A Look at the pictures. Read the conversation.

B Listen and read.

Diana: Is there an apartment for rent?
Manager: Yes, there is.
Diana: How many bedrooms are there?
Manager: Two.

C Listen again and repeat.

D Work with a partner. Practice the conversation. Use your own ideas.

A: Is there _____ for rent?

B: Yes, there is.

A: How many _____ are there?

B: _____.

Need help?

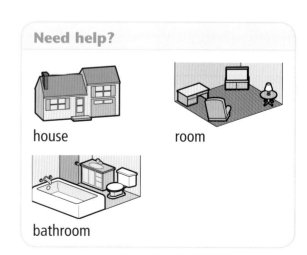

house   room

bathroom

2 Listen for housing information

🎧 **A** Listen and point to the rooms.

🎧 **B** Listen again. Number the homes.

_____

_____

_____

1

3 Real-life math

A Look at the picture. Read the words. Is the apartment cheap or expensive?

Apartment for Rent $900 a month

B Read the information. Do the math. Answer the question.

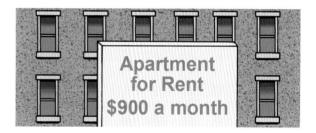

Rent is $900 a month. The first month you pay:
- the first month's rent, $900
- the last month's rent, $900

$900 + $900 = $_____

How much do you pay the first month for this apartment?

┌─ **TEST YOURSELF** ✓ ──────────────────

Copy the conversation. Close your book. Then add your own ideas and practice with a partner.

A: How many _____ are there?
B: _____.

1 Learn about types of housing

A Look at the pictures. Listen and repeat.

duplex

mobile home

rented room

B Listen. Circle *a* or *b*.

1. a. duplex   (b.) apartment
2. a. rented room   b. mobile home
3. a. house   b. mobile home
4. a. duplex   b. rented room
5. a. house   b. apartment

2 Get ready to read

A Look at the pictures. Read the abbreviations and the words.

apt = apartment

BR = bedroom

BA = bathroom

B Check (✔) the sentence about your home.

☐ I live in a one-bedroom home.

☐ I live in a two-bedroom home.

☐ I live in a three-bedroom home.

3 Read housing ads

A Read the housing ads.

①
RENT ME!
2 BR/1 BA apt.

31 Grant Street

$800 a month

②
New Home

3 BR/2 BA house

2627 Third Street

$1,200 a month

③
DUPLEX
1 BR/1 BA duplex

85 Second Street

$600 a month

④
Room for rent in a family home

$350 a month

Call: (787) 555-0923

B Look at the housing ads. Circle *yes* or *no*.

1. The house is on Grant Street.	yes	(no)
2. The apartment has two bedrooms.	yes	no
3. The duplex has two bathrooms.	yes	no
4. The apartment rent is $800 a month.	yes	no
5. The room for rent is $800 a month.	yes	no
6. The duplex is on Third Street.	yes	no

BRING IT TO LIFE

Bring in a housing ad from a newspaper or the Internet.
Circle 2 abbreviations.

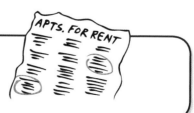

1 Grammar

A Look at the pictures. Complete the sentences.
Use the possessive.

Marco   Lee   Dara   Mr. and Mrs. Luna

1. ___Marco's___ bedroom is small.
2. _____ living room is big.

3. _____ refrigerator is yellow.
4. _____ car is blue.

B Look at the pictures in 1A. Complete the questions.

1. ___How many windows___ are there in Marco's bedroom?
2. _____ are there in Lee's living room?
3. _____ are there in Dara's kitchen?
4. _____ are there in Mr. and Mrs. Luna's garage?

2 Group work

A Work with 2–3 classmates. Look at the picture. Say what you see.

B Work with your group. Look at the picture in 2A again. Write what you see. Check your spelling in a dictionary.

1. _____bedroom_____ 4. _____

2. _____ 5. _____

3. _____ 6. _____

C Work with your classmates. Make a list of the words from 2B.

PROBLEM SOLVING

A Listen. Look at the pictures.

Mr. and Mrs. Kolda's Problem

B Work with your classmates. Help Mr. and Mrs. Kolda.

a. Light candles.   b. Call the electric company.

c. Call 911.   d. Other: _____

UNIT **12**

Yes, I can!

FOCUS ON
- jobs
- job skills
- *can* and *can't*
- job interviews
- reading a job ad

LESSON 1 Vocabulary

1 Learn the names of jobs

A Look at the pictures. Where are the people?

🎧 **B** Listen and point to the pictures.

🎧 **C** Listen and repeat the words.

1. gardener	4. cashier	7. truck driver
2. painter	5. hairdresser	8. secretary
3. housekeeper	6. mechanic	9. salesperson

D Read the new words with a partner.

2 Talk about jobs

A Look at the picture. Complete the words.

1. h a __i__ __r__ d r __e__ s __s__ e r

2. ____ a s h i ____ r

3. h ____ u s e ____ ____ e p e r

4. g a r ____ ____ n ____ r

5. s ____ ____ r e t ____ ____ y

6. p ____ ____ n t e ____

7. s a ____ e s p ____ ____ s o n

8. m ____ c ____ a ____ i c

9. t r ____ c k d r ____ ____ e r

B Listen and repeat.

1. **A:** Is she a salesperson?
   B: Yes, she is.

2. **A:** Is he a housekeeper?
   B: No, he isn't. He's a painter.

C Work with a partner. Point to the picture in 2A.
Practice the conversation.

A: Is _____ a _____?

B: _____.

TEST YOURSELF ✔

Close your book. Write 6 jobs. Check your spelling in a dictionary.

1 Read about job skills

A Look at the pictures. What jobs do you see?

B Listen and repeat the words.

1. cut hair
2. fix cars
3. drive a truck
4. paint houses
5. clean
6. sell clothes
7. take care of plants
8. use a computer

C Listen and read Nick's story.

1. My brother is a mechanic.
2. He can fix cars.
3. My friend is a truck driver.
4. She can drive a truck.
5. I want a job.

🎧 **D** Listen to Nora's story. Circle the correct word.

1. My friend is a ____.   (painter)   gardener

2. He can ____ houses.   clean   paint

3. My sister is a ____.   salesperson   secretary

4. She can ____ a computer.   fix   use

5. I ____ a job.   want   what

Nora

2 Write about job skills

A Write about job skills. Complete the sentences. Use your own ideas.

My _____ is a _____.

He can _____.

My _____ is a _____.

She can _____.

B Read your story to a partner.

3 Listen for job skills

🎧 **A** Listen and check the skills on the job applications.

① **Job Application**
Name: Lily Ng
Current job: secretary
Job skills:

☐ drive a car
☑ use a computer
☐ speak English
☐ other: _____

② **Job Application**
Name: Gabriela Valdez
Current job: hairdresser
Job skills:

☐ drive a car
☐ use a computer
☐ speak English
☐ other: _____

③ **Job Application**
Name: Paul Fields
Current job: truck driver
Job skills:

☐ drive a car
☐ use a computer
☐ speak English
☐ other: drive a truck

TEST YOURSELF ✔

Copy the sentences. Close your book. Then complete the sentences. Use your own ideas.

My friend is a _____. My friend can _____.

1 Learn statements with *can* and *can't*

A Look at the pictures. Read the sentences.

She can cut hair.

He can sell clothes.

He can't drive.

She can't fix computers.

B Study the charts. Listen and repeat.

I You He She It We They	can	cut hair.

I You He She It We They	can't	drive.

C Complete the sentences. Use *can* or *can't*. Then read the sentences with a partner.

1. He ____can't____ cut hair.

2. She _____ cut hair.

3. He _____ fix bicycles.

4. She _____ drive.

✔ Use *can* and *can't* to describe job skills

2 Learn *Yes/No* questions and answers with *can* and *can't*

A Look at the pictures. Read the conversations.

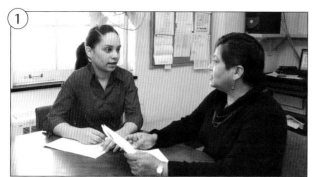

1

A: <u>Can you write</u> in English?
B: <u>Yes, I can.</u>

2

A: <u>Can you use</u> a computer?
B: <u>No, I can't.</u>

B Study the charts. Listen and repeat.

Can	you he she they	use a computer?

Yes,	I he she they	can.

No,	I he she they	can't.

C Complete the questions and answers. Use *can* or *can't*.

1. **A:** ___Can she___ use a computer?

   B: Yes, she can.

2. **A:** _____ write in English?

   B: No, he can't.

3. **A:** _____ fix computers?

   B: Yes, they can.

4. **A:** Can you sell clothes?

   B: No, I _____.

5. **A:** Can he drive a truck?

   B: Yes, he _____.

6. **A:** Can she paint houses?

   B: No, she _____.

D Work with a partner. Read the conversations in 2C.

TEST YOURSELF ✔

Write sentences with *can* and sentences with *can't*. Compare your sentences with a partner.

Jordan can sell clothes. Drew can't cut hair.

1 Learn to answer job-interview questions

A Look at the pictures. Read the conversation.

B Listen and read.

Patrick: Can you use a computer?
Silvia: Yes, I can.
Patrick: Can you work evenings?
Silvia: Yes, I can.

C Listen again and repeat.

D Work with a partner. Practice the conversation.
Use your own ideas.

A: Can you _____?

B: Yes, I can.

A: Can you _____?

B: Yes, I can.

2 Listen for a work schedule

🎧 **A** Listen. Point to the days Solana works.

Work Schedule: Solana Gilbert

	Mon.	Tues.	Wed.	Thurs.	Fri.	Sat.	Sun.
6 a.m.–12 p.m.	✔						
12 p.m.–6 p.m.							
6 p.m.–12 a.m.							

🎧 **B** Listen again. Check (✔) when Solana works.

3 Practice your pronunciation

🎧 **A** Listen for *can* and *can't*.

can	can't
I **can** drive.	I **can't** drive.
I **can** work.	I **can't** work.

🎧 **B** Listen and check (✔) *can* or *can't*.

	can	can't
1.	✔	
2.		
3.		
4.		
5.		
6.		

TEST YOURSELF ✔

Copy the conversation. Close your book. Then add your
own ideas and practice with a partner.

A: Can you _____?
B: _____.

1 Learn about more jobs

A Look at the pictures. Listen and repeat.

classroom aide
A classroom aide helps students.

babysitter
A babysitter takes care of children.

dental assistant
A dental assistant helps a dentist.

construction worker
A construction worker builds houses.

B Match.

_d_ 1. He builds houses.　　　　　a. babysitter

___ 2. She takes care of children.　　b. dental assistant

___ 3. He helps students.　　　　　c. classroom aide

___ 4. She helps a dentist.　　　　　d. construction worker

2 Get ready to read

A Look at the pictures. Read the words.

  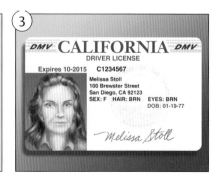

FT = full time = 40 hours per week

PT = part time

driver's license

B Circle *yes* or *no*. Use your own information.

Can you work full time?	yes	no
Can you work part time?	yes	no
Do you have a driver's license?	yes	no

3 Read job ads

A Read the job ads.

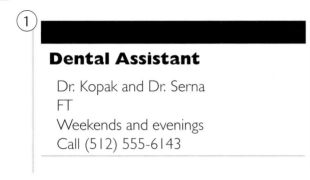

① **Dental Assistant**

Dr. Kopak and Dr. Serna
FT
Weekends and evenings
Call (512) 555-6143

② CONSTRUCTION WORKER

Acme Construction

PT
Mon., Wed., Fri. mornings
July/August
Call (512) 555-9090

③ *Babysitter*

Melrose Adult School

PT
Nights/Weekends
Driver's License
Call (891) 555-9870

④ **Classroom aide**

Hawaiian Gardens School

PT
Mornings, Mon.-Fri.
Call (989) 555-9870

B Look at the job ads. Check [✔] the correct ads.

	Ad 1	Ad 2	Ad 3	Ad 4
1. work on Saturdays	✔		✔	
2. work full time				
3. work July and August				
4. work in the morning				
5. have a driver's license				
6. work in the evening				

BRING IT TO LIFE

Bring a job ad from a newspaper or the Internet to class.
Circle 3 words you know.

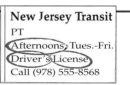

New Jersey Transit
PT
Afternoons, Tues.-Fri.
Driver's License
Call (978) 555-8568

1 Grammar

A **Complete the sentences. Use *can*.**

1. A babysitter ___can take care of children___.

2. A truck driver _____.

3. A hairdresser _____.

4. I _____.

B **Complete the questions and answers. Use *can* or *can't*.**

1. **A:** Can he fix the car?

   B: Yes, _____he can_____.

2. **A:** Can she work tonight?

   B: No, _____.

3. **A:** Can you use a computer?

   B: No, _____.

4. **A:** _____ drive?

   B: Yes, they can.

5. **A:** _____ paint houses?

   B: No, he can't.

6. **A:** _____ clean the house?

   B: Yes, she can.

2 Group work

A **Work with 2–3 classmates. Look at the picture. Say what you see.**

B Work with your group. Look at the picture in 2A again.
Write what you see. Check your spelling in a dictionary.

1. _____construction worker_____   4. _____

2. _____   5. _____

3. _____   6. _____

C Work with your classmates. Make a list of the words from 2B.

PROBLEM SOLVING

A Listen. Look at the pictures.

Adriana's Problem

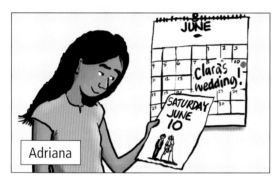

B Work with your classmates. Help Adriana.

a. Say, "I can't work Saturday. It's my friend's wedding."

b. Call in sick.

c. Go to work. Don't go to the wedding.

d. Other: _____

LISTENING SCRIPT

PRE-UNIT   The First Step

Pg. 3 Lesson 1—Exercise 1D

M = Man, W = Woman
 1. M: a
 2. W: i
 3. M: j
 4. W: h
 5. M: p
 6. W: n
 7. M: y
 8. W: f

Pg. 3 Lesson 1—Exercise 2A

W = Woman, M = Man
 1. W: Book. B-O-O-K. Book.
 2. M: Pen. P-E-N. Pen.
 3. W: Pencil. P-E-N-C-I-L. Pencil.
 4. M: Student. S-T-U-D-E-N-T. Student.
 5. W: Teacher. T-E-A-C-H-E-R. Teacher.
 6. M: Paper. P-A-P-E-R. Paper.

Pg. 4 Lesson 2—Exercise 1E

W = Woman, M = Man
 1. W: (212) 555-4261
 2. M: (629) 555-7583
 3. W: (748) 555-6932
 4. M: (256) 555-1407
 5. W: (387) 555-6340
 6. M: (512) 555-7928
 7. W: (936) 555-4821
 8. M: (481) 555-6017

UNIT 1   Nice to Meet You

Pg. 8 Lesson 1—Exercise 1B

W = Woman, M = Man
 1. M: open
 2. W: close
 3. M: circle
 4. W: say
 5. M: check
 6. W: sign

Pg. 9 Lesson 1—Exercise 2B

W = Woman, M = Man
 1. W: Close your book.
 2. M: Say *pencil*.
 3. W: Sign your name.
 4. M: Read number one.
 5. W: Circle your name.

Pg. 10 Lesson 2—Exercise 1D

M = Man
M: 1. My first name is Alan.
   2. My last name is Woo.
   3. I am a student.
   4. My teacher is Marsha Lee.

Pg. 11 Lesson 2—Exercise 3A

W = Woman, M = Man
W: What is your first name?
M: John.
W: What is your last name?
M: Wong.

Pg. 15 Lesson 4—Exercise 2A

M1 = Man 1, M2 = Man 2, M3 = Man 3, M4 = Man 4,
W1 = Woman 1, W2 = Woman 2, W3 = Woman 3
 1. M1: What's your name?
    W1: Mary. M-A-R-Y. Mary.
 2. W1: What's your name?
    W2: Joan. J-O-A-N. Joan.
 3. W2: What's your name?
    M2: Mel. M-E-L. Mel.
 4. M2: What's your name?
    W3: Sandy. S-A-N-D-Y. Sandy.
 5. W3: What's your name?
    M3: Jerry. J-E-R-R-Y. Jerry.
 6. M3: What's your name?
    M4: Corvin. C-O-R-V-I-N. Corvin.

Pg. 15 Lesson 4—Exercise 3B

W = Woman, M = Man
 1. W: meet
 2. M: nice
 3. W: write
 4. M: read

Pg. 16 Lesson 5—Exercise 1B

W = Woman, M = Man
 1. W: a notebook
 2. M: an eraser
 3. W: a binder
 4. M: an English dictionary
 5. W: a pen
 6. M: an open book
 7. W: an English class
 8. M: a teacher

Pg. 19 Problem Solving—Exercise A

W = Woman
W: Amaya is in class. She is writing. Uh-oh! Her pencil!

UNIT 2   How are you feeling?

Pg. 20 Lesson 1—Exercise 1B

W = Woman
W: 1. fine
   2. happy
   3. excited
   4. sad
   5. hungry
   6. thirsty
   7. tired
   8. sick

Pg. 23 Lesson 2—Exercise 3A

M = Man, W = Woman
M: Where are you from?
W: I am from Vietnam.
M: Where is Lian from?
W: She is from China.

Pg. 24 Lesson 3—Exercise 1B

M = Man, W = Woman
M: I am not tired.
W: You are not tired.
M: He is not tired.
W: She is not tired.
M: It is not tired.
W: We are not tired.
M: They are not tired.

Pg. 27 Lesson 4—Exercise 2A

M = Man, W = Woman
1. M: How are you feeling?
2. W: Where are you from?
3. M: What's your name?

Pg. 27 Lesson 4—Exercise 2B

M = Man, W = Woman
1. M: How are you feeling?
2. W: What's your name?
3. M: How are you feeling?
4. W: Where are you from?

Pg. 31 Problem Solving—Exercise A

M = Man
M: From Gary Prajak. Four-fifty-three Hill Street,
    Los Angeles, California, 91324.
    To Emily Prajak, forty-nine eighty-seven Broad Street,
    Boston, Massachusetts. 02901? 02109? 02190? What's
    the zip code?

UNIT 3   What time is it?

Pg. 32 Lesson 1—Exercise 1B

W = Woman, M = Man
1. W: morning
2. M: afternoon
3. W: evening
4. M: night
5. W: 2:00
6. M: 2:15
7. W: 2:30
8. M: 2:45
9. W: noon
10. M: midnight

Pg. 35 Lesson 2—Exercise 1D

M = Man
M: 1. I go to school at 9:00.
    2. I go to the library at 1:00.
    3. I go to English class at 2:30.
    4. I go to work at 6:00.

Pg. 35 Lesson 2—Exercise 3B

M = Man, W = Woman
1. M: It's 7 a.m.
2. W: It's 7 p.m.
3. M: It's 9 p.m.
4. W: It's 10 a.m.

Pg. 36 Lesson 3—Exercise 1B

M = Man, W = Woman
M: Is he at school?
W: Is she at school?
M: Is it 6:00?
W: Are you at home?
M: Are they at home?

Pg. 39 Lesson 4—Exercise 2A

M1 = Man 1, M2 = Man 2, M3 = Man 3, M4 = Man 4,
W1 = Woman 1, W2 = Woman 2, W3 = Woman 3,
W4 = Woman 4
1. M1: Hi. Is the school open?
    W1: Yes, it is. We open at 10 a.m.
2. M2: Hello. Is the clinic open?
    W2: No, it's not. We open at 8:00 in the morning.
3. W3: Is the library open at 9 p.m.?
    M3: No, I'm sorry. It's closed.
4. W4: Hi. Is the store open at 10 in the evening?
    M4: Yes, it is.

Pg. 40 Lesson 5—Exercise 1B

W = Woman, M = Man
1. W: Excuse me, what time is the bus to Salem?
2. M: Where is the train to Springfield?
3. W: My car is at home.
4. M: The plane is here.

Pg. 43 Problem Solving—Exercise A

M = Man
M: Go to the clinic at 10:00 a.m. My English class is
    from 9 a.m. to 12 p.m. Hmmm…

UNIT 4   What day is it?

Pg. 44 Lesson 1—Exercise 1B

W = Woman
W: 1. Sunday
   2. Monday
   3. Tuesday
   4. Wednesday
   5. Thursday
   6. Friday
   7. Saturday
   8. day
   9. week
   10. today
   11. tomorrow
   12. weekend

Pg. 47 Lesson 2—Exercise 1D

M = Man
M: 1. It's April.
   2. Next month is May.
   3. My birthday is in July.

Pg. 47 Lesson 2—Exercise 3B

W = Woman, M = Man
1. W: 1946
2. M: 2008
3. W: 1985
4. M: 1972
5. W: May
6. M: February 1965

Pg. 48 Lesson 3—Exercise 1B

M = Man, W = Woman
M: The birthday party is on Tuesday at 7:00.
W: The class party is on Thursday at 5:00.

Pg. 48 Lesson 3—Exercise 1D

W = Woman, M = Man
1. W: It's on Wednesday.
2. M: It's at 12:30.
3. W: It's at 6:00.
4. M: It's on Tuesday.
5. W: It's at 9:45.
6. M: The class is on Friday morning.
7. W: The party is at 9:00.
8. M: The party is on Saturday.

Pg. 49 Lesson 3—Exercise 2B

A = Abena, G = Gloria
A: When is the birthday party?
G: It's on Tuesday.
A: Where is the party?
G: It's at my house.
A: What time is the party?
G: It's at 6:00.

Pg. 51 Lesson 4—Exercise 2B

W = Woman, M = Man
1. W: four-six-1999
2. M: seven-twelve-1960
3. W: nine-eleven-1982
4. M: ten-eight-2009
5. W: two-one-2007
6. M: five-three-1951
7. W: five-eleven-1974
8. M: eight-one-2008

Pg. 51 Lesson 4—Exercise 3C

W = Woman, M = Man
1. W: Tuesday
2. M: Thursday
3. W: twenty
4. M: thirteen
5. W: teacher
6. M: three

Pg. 55 Problem Solving—Exercise A

W = Woman
W: English class registration is on Tuesday, September 3rd, from 8 a.m. to 10 a.m.
   Today is Tuesday, September 3rd. Oh, no! It's ten o'clock now!

UNIT 5   How much is it?

Pg. 56 Lesson 1—Exercise 1B

M = Man, W = Woman
1. M: bills
2. W: dollar
3. M: coins
4. W: cents
5. M: penny
6. W: nickel
7. M: dime
8. W: quarter

Pg. 57 Lesson 1—Exercise 2C

M = Man, W = Woman
1. M: seventy-five cents
2. W: two dollars
3. M: thirty-five cents
4. W: sixteen dollars
5. M: seven dollars
6. W: eighty cents

Pg. 59 Lesson 2—Exercise 1D

M = Man
M: 1. Shoe World is a good store.
   2. The shoes are good.
   3. The socks are cheap.

Pg. 59 Lesson 2—Exercise 3B

M = Man, W = Woman
1. M: Three dollars and twenty-five cents
2. W: Four dollars and fifty-two cents
3. M: Eight dollars and ninety-one cents
4. W: Six dollars and thirty-seven cents
5. M: Five dollars and forty-nine cents
6. W: Two dollars and seventy-four cents

Pg. 63 Lesson 4—Exercise 2B

W = Woman, M = Man
1. W: Your change is thirty-five cents.
2. M: That's seven cents change.
3. W: Your change is twenty-five cents.
4. M: That's sixteen cents change.
5. W: That's one dollar and ten cents change.
6. M: That's seven dollars change.

Pg. 64 Lesson 5—Exercise 1B

M = Man, W = Woman
1. M: a check
2. W: a money order
3. M: a debit card
4. W: cash

Pg. 67 Problem Solving—Exercise A

M = Man
M: Twenty dollars and fifteen cents. These shoes are cheap! Twenty dollars and five cents. Uh oh!

UNIT 6 That's My Son

Pg. 68 Lesson 1—Exercise 1B

W = Woman, M = Man
1. W: parents
2. M: mother
3. W: father
4. M: baby
5. W: girl
6. M: boy
7. W: friend
8. M: husband
9. W: wife

Pg. 71 Lesson 2—Exercise 1D

M = Man
M: 1. These are my children.
   2. This is my daughter.
   3. She's twenty years old.
   4. This is my son.
   5. He's fifteen years old.

Pg. 71 Lesson 2—Exercise 3B

M1 = Man 1, M2 = Man 2, W1 = Woman 1,
W2 = Woman 2
1. M1: I'm divorced.
2. W1: I'm married.
3. M2: I'm single.
4. W2: I'm divorced.

Pg. 73 Lesson 3—Exercise 2B

M = Man, W = Woman
M: I live in New York.
W: You live in New York.
M: He lives in New York.
W: She lives in New York.
M: We live in New York.
W: They live in New York.

Pg. 75 Lesson 4—Exercise 2B

M = Man, W1 = Woman 1, W2 = Woman 2,
W3 = Woman 3
1. M: I'm Mr. Jones.
2. W1: I'm Miss Wong.
3. W2: I'm Ms. Park.
4. W3: I'm Mrs. Chavez.

Pg. 79 Problem Solving—Exercise A

M = Man
M: Rosa's son is in fourth grade. He is not a good student. He plays baseball every day. He is very good at baseball.

UNIT 7 Do we need apples?

Pg. 80 Lesson 1—Exercise 1B

M = Man, W = Woman
1. M: fruit
2. W: bananas
3. M: apples
4. W: grapes
5. M: oranges
6. W: vegetables
7. M: broccoli
8. W: cabbage
9. M: corn

Pg. 83 Lesson 2—Exercise 1D

M = Man
M: 1. I like meat.
   2. I don't like cheese.
   3. My wife likes lamb.
   4. My son likes eggs.
   5. We all like bread.

Pg. 83 Lesson 2—Exercise 3A

M = Man, W = Woman
1. M: Pork is meat.
2. W: Grapes are fruit.
3. M: Cabbage is a vegetable.

Pg. 83 Lesson 2—Exercise 3B

W = Woman, M = Man
1. W: It's a vegetable.
2. M: It's meat.
3. W: It's fruit.
4. M: It's a vegetable.
5. W: It's fruit.
6. M: It's a vegetable.

Pg. 84 Lesson 3—Exercise 1B

M = Man, W = Woman
M: I don't like cabbage.
W: You don't like cabbage.
M: He doesn't like cabbage.
W: She doesn't like cabbage.
M: We don't like cabbage.
W: They don't like cabbage.

Pg. 87 Lesson 4—Exercise 2A

W = Woman
W: United Supermarket Sale!
    Bananas are twenty-nine cents a pound.
    Oranges are one dollar and fifty cents a pound.
    Grapes are one dollar and ten cents a pound.
    Apples are three dollars and eighty-seven cents a
    pound.

Pg. 88 Lesson 5—Exercise 1B

M = Man, W = Woman
  1. M: a can of soup
  2. W: a box of cereal
  3. M: a bottle of juice
  4. W: a can of coffee
  5. M: a bottle of water
  6. W: a box of tea

Pg. 91 Problem Solving—Exercise A

W = Woman
W: Duncan eats breakfast at six o'clock in the morning.
    He has donuts and coffee. Duncan eats lunch at the
    office. He eats pizza. Duncan eats a hamburger at
    night.

UNIT 8   Take Two Tablets

Pg. 92 Lesson 1—Exercise 1B

M = Man, W = Woman
  1. M: head
  2. W: eye
  3. M: ear
  4. W: nose
  5. M: arm
  6. W: stomach
  7. M: hand
  8. W: leg
  9. M: foot

Pg. 95 Lesson 2—Exercise 1D

M = Man
M: 1. My family is sick.
    2. My brother has a fever.
    3. My sister has a stomachache.
    4. My mother has a cough.
    5. I have a cold.

Pg. 95 Lesson 2—Exercise 3A

D = Doctor, W = Woman, M = Man
  1. D: What's the matter today, Mrs. Lopez?
     W: Oh, I have a cough, a fever, and a sore throat.
     D: Anything else?
     W: Yes, I have a stomachache, too!
  2. D: What's the matter today, Mr. Foss?
     M: Oh, I have a headache and an earache.
     D: Anything else?
     M: Yes, I have a sore throat, too.

Pg. 96 Lesson 3—Exercise 1B

M = Man, W = Woman
M: I have the flu.
W: You have the flu.
M: He has the flu.
W: She has the flu.
M: We have the flu.
W: They have the flu.

Pg. 99 Lesson 4—Exercise 2A

WR = Woman Receptionist, W1 = Woman 1,
W2 = Woman 2, M1 = Man 1, M2 = Man 2
  1. W1: Hi. This is Berta Sanchez. I need to see the
          doctor. I have a stomachache.
     WR: Is Wednesday at eight o'clock OK?
     W1: Wednesday at eight o'clock? Yes, that's fine.
          Thank you.
  2. M1: Hi. This is Vincent Wu. I need to see the doctor.
          I have a sore throat.
     WR: Is Wednesday at 8:30 OK?
     M1: Wednesday at 8:30? Yes, thank you.
  3. M2: Hi. This is Mr. Cabrera. My son needs to see the
          doctor. He has a cough.
     WR: Is Thursday at 9:00 OK?
     M2: OK. See you Thursday at 9:00.
  4. W2: Hi. This is Tan Nguyen. I need to see the doctor.
          I have a headache.
     WR: How about Friday at 9:30?
     W2: Friday at 9:30? Well, OK.

Pg. 103 Problem Solving—Exercise A

W = Woman
W: Time for work. Oh, no! I have a cold. 98.6 degrees.
    Well, I don't have a fever. That's good.

UNIT 9   What size?

Pg. 104 Lesson 1—Exercise 1B

M = Man, W = Woman
  1. M: black
  2. W: white
  3. M: red
  4. W: blue
  5. M: yellow
  6. W: green
  7. M: brown
  8. W: orange
  9. M: purple

Pg. 107 Lesson 2—Exercise 1D

M = Man
M: 1. It's January.
    2. I'm wearing a blue coat.
    3. I'm wearing brown boots.
    4. I'm wearing a brown belt.

Pg. 107 Lesson 2—Exercise 3A

W = Woman, M = Man
  1. W: She's wearing a red dress.
  2. M: She's wearing an orange jacket.
  3. W: He's wearing a black coat.
  4. M: He's wearing blue shorts.

Pg. 108 Lesson 3—Exercise 1B

M = Man, W = Woman
M: I am wearing shoes.
W: You are wearing shoes.
M: He is wearing shoes.
W: She is wearing shoes.
M: It is wearing shoes.
W: We are wearing shoes.
M: They are wearing shoes.

Pg. 111 Lesson 4—Exercise 2B

M = Man, W = Woman
1. M: I'm looking for a blue T-shirt, size extra-large.
2. W: I'm looking for a yellow T-shirt, size medium.
3. M: I'm looking for a green T-shirt, size large.
4. W: I'm looking for a purple T-shirt, size extra-large.

Pg. 111 Lesson 4—Exercise 2C

WC = Woman Customer, MS = Man Salesclerk
1. WC: How much is the blue T-shirt?
   MS: It's twelve dollars and ninety-nine cents.
2. WC: How much are the black boots?
   MS: They're forty dollars.
3. WC: How much is the orange jacket?
   MS: It's twenty-five dollars.
4. WC: How much is the extra-large T-shirt?
   MS: It's fourteen dollars and ninety-nine cents.
5. WC: How much is the orange coat?
   MS: It's fifty-three dollars.
6. WC: How much are the brown boots?
   MS: They're eighty-seven dollars.

Pg. 115 Problem Solving—Exercise A

M = Man
M: Today is Ethan's birthday. Ethan's wife is giving him a present. It's a shirt. It's green, yellow, and red. Uh oh.

UNIT 10 Where's the bank?

Pg. 116 Lesson 1—Exercise 1B

W = Woman, M = Man
1. W: bookstore
2. M: bus station
3. W: drugstore
4. M: laundromat
5. W: park
6. M: bank
7. W: post office
8. M: restaurant
9: W: supermarket

Pg. 119 Lesson 2—Exercise 1D

M = Man
M: 1. My house is on Third Street.
   2. There is a park next to the house.
   3. There is a post office across from the park.
   4. There is a bank on the corner.
   5. I go to the bookstore on Sundays.

Pg. 119 Lesson 2—Exercise 3A

W = Woman, M = Man
1. W: The park is next to the house.
2. M: The laundromat is across from the apartment building.
3. W: The house is between the park and the apartment building.
4. M: The park is on the corner.

Pg. 120 Lesson 3—Exercise 1B

W = Woman, M = Man
W: There is a supermarket on Green Street.
M: There is a post office on Green Street.
W: There are two banks on Green Street.
M: There are three restaurants on Green Street.

Pg. 123 Lesson 4—Exercise 2A

W = Woman, M = Man
1. M: The drugstore is on the corner of First Street and Washington Street.
2. W: The restaurant is on the corner of Second Street and Washington Street.
3. M: The park is on Elm Street between First Street and Second Street.
4. W: The bookstore is on Second Street between Elm Street and Washington Street.

Pg. 124 Lesson 5—Exercise 1B

W = Woman, M = Man
1. M: Go to the fire station.
2. W: Get an ambulance!
3. W: Call the police station.
4. M: Go to the DMV.

Pg. 127 Problem Solving—Exercise A

M = Man
M: Elena is a student. It's 11 p.m. She is studying. She is not happy about the music.

UNIT 11 This Is My Home

Pg. 128 Lesson 1—Exercise 1B

M = Man, W = Woman
1. M: room
2. W: window
3. M: furniture
4. W: sofa
5. M: bed
6. W: dresser
7. M: TV
8. W: stove
9. M: refrigerator

Pg. 131 Lesson 2—Exercise 1D

W = Woman
W: 1. This is my home.
   2. There are three bedrooms.
   3. There is a table in the kitchen.
   4. There is a window above the table.
   5. I like my living room.

Pg. 131　Lesson 2—Exercise 3A

W = Woman
W: There is a desk below the window. There is a dresser next to the desk. There is a bed next to the dresser. There is a clock above the bed. There are two books on the desk.

Pg. 133　Lesson 3—Exercise 2B

M = Man, W = Woman
M: How many chairs are there in the living room?
W: How many windows are there in the living room?

Pg. 135　Lesson 4—Exercise 2A

M = Man, W = Woman
1. M: There are two bedrooms and one bathroom. The bathroom is between the bedrooms.
2. W: There are two bedrooms and one bathroom. The bathroom is next to the living room.
3. M: There is one bedroom and one bathroom. The bathroom is next to the bedroom.
4. W: There are two bedrooms and two bathrooms. One bathroom is next to the kitchen. One bathroom is between the bedrooms.

Pg. 136　Lesson 5—Exercise 1B

W1 = Woman 1, W2 = Woman 2, W3 = Woman 3,
M1 = Man 1, M2 = Man 2
1. W1: I live in an apartment.
2. M1: I live in a rented room.
3. W2: I live in a mobile home.
4. M2: I live in a duplex.
5. W3: I live in a house.

Pg. 139　Problem Solving—Exercise A

W = Woman
W: Mr. and Mrs. Kolda are eating dinner. Oh, no! The lights are off. The lights are off in their house. The lights are off on their street.

UNIT 12　Yes, I can!

Pg. 140　Lesson 1—Exercise 1B

M = Man, W = Woman
1. M: gardener
2. W: painter
3. M: housekeeper
4. W: cashier
5. M: hairdresser
6. W: mechanic
7. M: truck driver
8. W: secretary
9. M: salesperson

Pg. 143　Lesson 2—Exercise 1D

W = Woman
W: 1.　My friend is a painter.
　　2.　He can paint houses.
　　3.　My sister is a secretary.
　　4.　She can use a computer.
　　5.　I want a job.

Pg. 143　Lesson 2—Exercise 3A

W1 = Woman 1, W2 = Woman 2, M = Man
1. W1: My name is Lily Ng. I'm a secretary. I can use a computer and speak English.
2. W2: I'm Gabriela Valdez. I am a hairdresser. I can cut hair.
3. M:　My name is Paul Fields. I am a truck driver. I can drive a car or a truck. I can also speak English.

Pg. 144　Lesson 3—Exercise 1B

W = Woman, M = Man
W: I can cut hair.
M: You can cut hair.
W: He can cut hair.
M: She can cut hair.
W: It can cut hair.
M: We can cut hair.
W: They can cut hair.

W: I can't drive.
M: You can't drive.
W: He can't drive.
M: She can't drive.
W: It can't drive.
M: We can't drive.
W: They can't drive.

Pg. 145　Lesson 3—Exercise 2B

M = Man, W = Woman
M: Can you use a computer?
W: Can he use a computer?
M: Can she use a computer?
W: Can they use a computer?

M: Yes, I can.
W: Yes, he can.
M: Yes, she can.
W: Yes, they can.

M: No, I can't.
W: No, he can't.
M: No, she can't.
W: No, they can't.

Pg. 147 Lesson 4—Exercise 2A

W = Woman
W: Solana works Monday, Tuesday, Wednesday, Saturday, and Sunday.
  On Monday she works from 6 a.m. to 12 p.m.
  On Tuesday she works from 6 a.m. to 12 p.m.
  On Wednesday she works from 12 p.m. to 6 p.m.
  On Saturday she works from 12 p.m. to 6 p.m.
  On Sunday she works from 12 p.m. to 6 p.m.
  She doesn't work on Thursday or Friday.

Pg. 147 Lesson 4—Exercise 3B

M1 = Man 1, M2 = Man 2, M3 = Man 3, W1 = Woman 1,
W2 = Woman 2, W3 = Woman 3
1. W1: I can drive.
2. M1: I can't drive.
3. W2: I can work.
4. M2: I can't work.
5. W3: I can't fix cars.
6. M3: I can fix cars.

Pg. 151 Problem Solving—Exercise A

W = Woman
W: Adriana's friend is getting married on Saturday.
  Adriana works in an office. Her boss says, "See you on
  Saturday at 9:00."

GRAMMAR CHARTS

THE SIMPLE PRESENT WITH *BE*

Statements

I	am	
You	are	a student.
He She	is	
It	is	a book.
We You They	are	students.

Negative statements

I	am not	
You	are not	a student.
He She	is not	
It	is not	a book.
We You They	are not	students.

Contractions

I am = I'm	I am not = I'm not
you are = you're	you are not = you're not
he is = he's	he is not = he's not
she is = she's	she is not = she's not
it is = it's	it is not = it's not
we are = we're	we are not = we're not
they are = they're	they are not = they're not

Yes/No questions

Am	I	
Are	you	
Is	he she it	at school?
Are	we you they	

Answers

	I	am.
	you	are.
Yes,	he she it	is.
	we you they	are.

	I	'm not.
	you	're not.
No,	he she it	's not.
	we you they	're not.

Information questions

Where	am	I?
How	are	you?
How Where Who	is	he? she?
How long How much What What time When Where Who	is	it?
Where	are	we? you? they?

THE PRESENT CONTINUOUS

Statements

I	am	
You	are	
He She It	is	sleeping.
We You They	are	

Negative statements

I	am not	
You	are not	
He She It	is not	sleeping.
We You They	are not	

Yes/No questions

Am	I	
Are	you	
Is	he she it	sleeping?
Are	we you they	

Answers

	I	am.		I	'm not.
	you	are.		you	're not.
Yes,	he she it	is.	No,	he she it	's not.
	we you they	are.		we you they	're not.

THE SIMPLE PRESENT

Statements

I You	like	
He She It	likes	rice.
We You They	like	

Negative Statements

I You	don't		
He She It	doesn't	like	rice.
We You They	don't		

Contractions

do not = don't
does not = doesn't

Yes/No questions

Do	I you		
Does	he she it	like	rice?
Do	we you they		

Answers

	I you	do.		I you	don't.
Yes,	he she it	does.	No,	he she it	doesn't.
	we you they	do.		we you they	don't.

CAN

Statements		
I You He She It We You They	can	work.

Negative Statements		
I You He She It We You They	can't	work.

Contraction
cannot = can't

Yes/No questions		
Can	I you he she it we you they	work?

Answers					
Yes,	I you he she it we you they	can.	No,	I you he she it we you they	can't.

THERE IS/THERE ARE

Statements			
There	is	a supermarket a drugstore	on First Street.
	are	two banks three restaurants	

Yes/No questions		
Is	there	a post office nearby? a laundromat nearby?

Questions with *How many*			
How many	bedrooms bathrooms	are	there?

THIS, THAT, THESE, AND THOSE

Singular Statements		Notes
This That	shirt is $35.	Use *this* and *that* when the people or things are near.

Plural Statements		Notes
These Those	pants are $14.	Use *these* and *those* when the people or things are far.

A AND AN

Articles	
a	pencil binder
an	eraser open book

PLURAL NOUNS

To make plural nouns	Examples	
For most nouns, add -s.	student—students	orange—oranges
If nouns end in -s, -sh, -ch, -x, add -es.	bus—buses	box—boxes
If nouns end in consonant + y, change –y to –ies.	family—families	country—countries
If nouns end in vowel + y, keep –y and add -s.	boy—boys	day—days
Some plural nouns do not end in -s, -es, or -ies. They are irregular plurals.	child—children man—men	person—people woman—women

SUBJECT PRONOUNS

Subject pronouns
I
you
he
she
it
we
you
they

POSSESSIVE ADJECTIVES

Possessive Adjectives
my
your
his
her
its
our
your
their

POSSESSIVES

Nouns		Notes
Gloria's Mr. and Mrs. Smith's	home is big.	For two or more nouns together, add -'s after the last noun.

PREPOSITIONS

Times and dates		Notes
The party is	on Tuesday. on Thursday.	Use *on* for days and dates. Use *at* for times.
	at 6:00. at 7:00.	

Locations			
The school	is	on	Pine Street.
		across from next to	the bus station.
		between	the post office and the park.
		on the corner.	
The sofa	is	in	the living room.
		below	the window.
The window		above	the sofa.

FREQUENCY AND TIME EXPRESSIONS

Frequency expressions		
Take two tablets	every twice a three times a	day.
	every four hours. every six hours.	

VOCABULARY LIST

A

above	130
across from	118
address	28
adult school	16
afternoon	32
ambulance	124
apartment	136
apartment building	118
apples	80
April	46
arm	92
ask	19
August	46

B

baby	68
babysitter	148
bananas	80
bank	116
bathroom	130
bed	128
bedroom	130
beef	82
below	130
belt	106
between	118
big	132
bills	56
binder	16
birthday	46
birthplace	22
black	104
blue	104
book	3
bookstore	116
boots	106
bottle	88
box	88
boy	68
bread	82
bring	16
broccoli	80
brother	70
brown	104
bus	40
bus station	116
buy	67

C

cabbage	80
calendar	52
call 911	139
call in sick	151

call the police	127
call the school	55
can	88
cap	106
car	40
cash	64
cashier	140
cents	56
cereal	88
chair	7
cheap	58
check (verb)	8
check (noun)	64
cheese	82
chicken	82
child	70
children	70
circle	8
city	22
classroom aide	148
clean	142
clock	7
close	8
clothes	58
cloudy	112
coat	106
coffee	88
coins	56
cold (noun)	94
cold (adj)	112
color	104
come	76
construction worker	148
cool	112
corn	80
cough	94
count	2
country	22
courthouse	124
credit card	64
cut hair	142

D

daughter	70
day	44
debit card	64
December	46
dental assistant	148
Department of Motor Vehicles (DMV)	124
desk	7
dictionary	16
dime	56
directory	124

divorced	71
do homework	76
dollar	56
dress	106
dresser	128
drive a truck	142
driver's license	148
drugstore	116
duplex	136

E

ear	92
earache	94
eat	91
eggs	82
electric bill	64
elementary school	76
email address	124
emergency	124
envelope	28
eraser	16
evening	32
every day	76
every four hours	100
every six hours	100
excited	20
expensive	58
extra-large	110
eye	92

F

father	68
February	46
fever	94
fine	20
fire station	124
first name	10
fix cars	142
flu	94
foot	92
form	28
Friday	44
friend	68
fruit	80
full time	148
furniture	128

G

garage	130
gardener	140
gas bill	64
girl	68
go home	34
go out	127

sofa	128
son	70
sore throat	94
soup	88
spell	2
state	22
stay home	103
stomach	92
stomachache	94
stove	128
student	3
Sunday	44
sunny	112
supermarket	116
supplies	16
sweater	58

T

table	7
tablespoon	100
tablet	100
take care of plants	142
talk	79
tea	88
teacher	3
teaspoon	100
telephone number	4
thanks	50
thirsty	20
three times a day	100
Thursday	44
tired	20
today	44
tomorrow	44
train	40
truck driver	140
T-shirt	106
Tuesday	44
TV	128
twice a day	100

U

use a computer	142

V

vegetables	80

W

walk	91
warm	112
water	88
wear	108
weather	112
Wednesday	44
week	44
weekend	44
white	104
wife	68
window	128
winter break	52
woman	5
work	2
write	2

Y

year	46
yellow	104

Z

zip code	28

INDEX

ACADEMIC SKILLS

Writing

CIVICS

LIFE SKILLS

Consumer Education

Environment and the World

Family and Parenting

Government and Community Resources

Health and Nutrition

Interpersonal Communication

Safety and Security

Telephone

Time and Money

Transportation and Travel

TOPICS

WORKFORCE SKILLS

Obtaining Employment

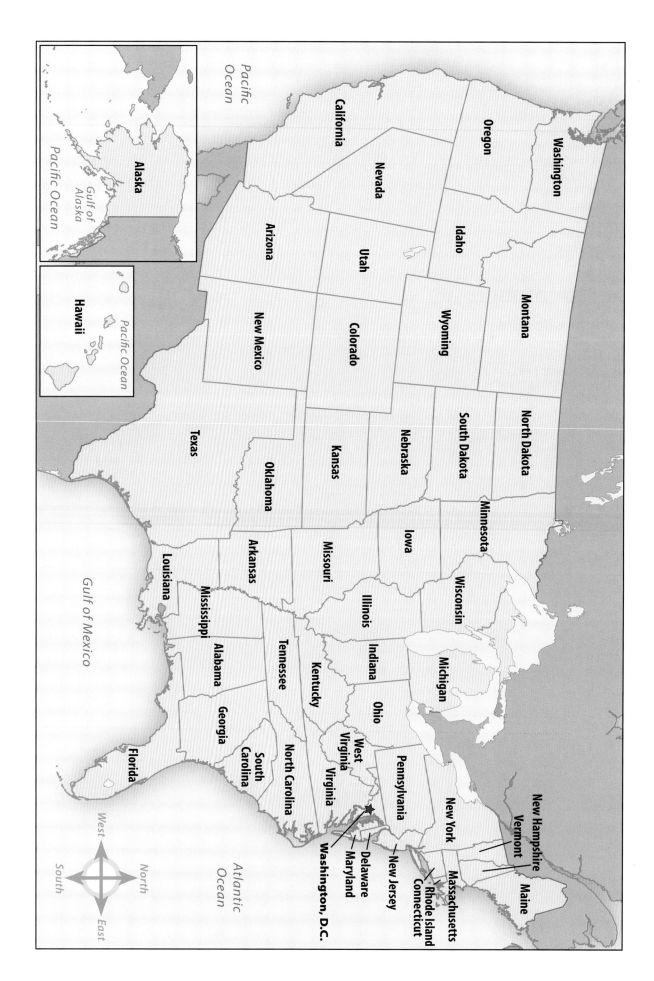